SY 0091066 X

D0120114

X

ST. JOSEPH'S T. COLLEGE

943.053

PALM

016590

ST. JOSEPH'S COLLEGE OF EDUCATION LIBRARY

This book is issued in accordance with current College
Library Regulations.

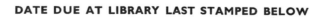

DATE DUE AT LIBRARY LAST STAMPED BELOW

-7 AUG. 1980
-8. JUL. 1986

GREAT LIVES

Frederick the Great

OVERLEAF LEFT Frederick the Great as the
Crown Prince, painted by his architect
and friend, Knobelsdorff.
RIGHT A statue of a musician from the
Chinese pavilion at Sans Souci.

G. W. von Knobelsdorff

Profilbildnis Friedrichs d. Gr. als Kronprinz

GREAT LIVES

Frederick the Great

Alan Palmer

Introduction by Elizabeth Longford

Weidenfeld and Nicolson London

© George Weidenfeld and Nicolson
and Book Club Associates 1974

All rights reserved. No part
of this publication may be
reproduced, stored in a
retrieval system, or
transmitted, in any form or
by any means, electronic,
mechanical, photocopying,
recording, or otherwise,
without the prior written
permission of the copyright
owner.

House editor Simon Dally
Art editor Andrew Shoolbred
Layout by Florianne Henfield

Filmset and printed by Cox & Wyman Ltd,
London, Fakenham and Reading

ST. JOSEPH'S COLLEGE OF EDUCATION
TRENCH HOUSE
BELFAST 11

Contents

Introduction

A LEADER WHO IS LABELLED 'The Great', by right of conquest alone, does not automatically win our allegiance today. We tend to look for other qualities besides military success. With Alexander and Catherine II, for instance, – both 'Greats' – posterity's imagination has been captured as much by their personalities as their deeds. The same is amply true of Frederick the Great.

It is nothing new to find genius allied to suffering. But Frederick's monstrous suffering in youth at the hands of his father, has to be seen to be believed. A well-documented story is a form of 'seeing'. And this is exactly what Alan Palmer gives us.

Frederick's was a male-dominated universe, of the kind from which philosopher-kings had always been expected to arise. We wonder, nevertheless, how far he was a dedicated woman-hater. Alan Palmer's account of his devotion to his clever sister and rejection of his plump wife forms a fascinating side-theme. It is rendered even more intriguing by Frederick's enchantment with music, literature and eighteenth-century painting: what Alan Palmer calls 'the exquisite sensitivity to feminine tenderness' of his Watteaus and Lancrets. Frederick chose to operate against a background of pink-and-blue paradises inhabited by frilly ladies on swings. Perhaps they were an antidote to the formidable historic background of real-life Empresses. Yet his happiest world was always masculine, in a Greek sense. Substitute Voltaire and Frederick for Aristotle and Alexander, or Socrates and Plato, and you have a Franco–German symposium at the palace of Sans Souci.

Frederick's wars can only too easily dissolve on the printed page into a jumble of gigantic grenadiers, impenetrable forests and miasmal marshes. But Alan Palmer is a brilliant general of his facts. Tumultuous events emerge for our benefit in a state of miraculous discipline, so that Frederick's many 'rendez-vous with glory' take shape for our consummate admiration, if not delight. But the delight is not wanting. For Frederick's great building operations give a lift to his victories. 'Buildings are my dolls', he once said. However severely we may judge Prussian expansionism, Frederick's ambition to serve and educate his people, and to create a splendid Berlin, was no mean one.

We see Frederick as a child of the 'Enlightenment', a conscious product of the Age of Reason. He believed intensely in science and learning, and in God not at all. But like so many children of the 'Enlightenment', he possessed little of its recommended rationality and calm. As Alan Palmer shows us, Frederick could be intolerably waspish even with those he loved. Far from displaying the classical *Mens sana in corpore sano*, his strange mind was encased in an undersized body, which he in turn draped in shabby clothes. A man who could drink champagne in cold coffee was clearly no Renaissance prince. Rather, a Gothic gnome from the roots of some German mountain. Tragically, also, the influence he exerted after his death was on the side of extremes, rather than of his own more modest idea of limited conquest. From among his most famous posthumous admirers, he might have accepted Bismarck and Kaiser William II, but Hitler – never!

At his accession he had described the crown as 'merely a hat that lets the rain in'. This was Frederick at his 'enlightened' best. Before his death he had reverted to the same detachment. His was the 'hollow crown' of Shakespeare's Richard II, in which Death kept his court, 'grinning at his pomp'.

Between his personally unhappy beginnings and his sardonic end, came the public years of resounding victory. After Frederick, Europe was never to be the same again. His tomb became an object of pilgrimage by almost all the great subsequent aggressors.

Elizabeth Longford

Seine Majestät
der König
mit Dero Suite

1 The Poor Soldie

Fritz

ON 18 JANUARY 1701 A UNIQUE CEREMONY TOOK PLACE in the audience chamber of the royal castle at Königsberg in East Prussia. The Elector Frederick III, head of the House of Hohenzollern and for the past thirteen years ruler over the Mark of Brandenburg and ducal Prussia, placed upon his brow a golden, diamond-studded crown and was duly hailed by the assembled burghers and courtiers as the first 'King of Prussia'. This simple act of self-coronation was followed by an elaborate service in the castle chapel. As artillery salutes shattered the white stillness of the Baltic city, the newest of Europe's monarchies enthroned its sovereign with all the pomp and reverence of an ancient tradition. No rite was neglected; the King was even anointed with consecrated oil by the chief pastors of the Lutheran and Calvinist Churches, created Bishops for the occasion. 'May Fortune smile upon our King, Frederick I', the Lutheran Bishop supplicated, 'May his throne become mightier and mightier, and may his children's children reign for ever in the Peace of Olden Israel.' 'Amen, Amen', responded the congregation fervently, while the choir sang a coronation anthem based on the twenty-first psalm. It was a jubilant note on which to welcome the eighteenth century, but an appropriate one. For eleven years later a son was born to the King's eldest son and baptized Frederick in his grandfather's honour, and before the century had run half its course this 'child of a child' was to astonish all Germany by his genius and shake the European dynasties by his will to make Prussia a great power.

Hitherto no impartial observer had rated the Hohenzollerns highly among the princely families of the continent. Although they claimed descent from one of Charlemagne's generals and had mastered the unruly barons of central Germany in the fifteenth century, their lands remained an essentially feudal heritage, sprawling haphazardly between the Rhine and the Niemen without any organic connection, like arable strips scattered in some vast medieval open field. It was only in 1640, when King Frederick I's father, Frederick William, became Elector of Brandenburg–Prussia that the fortunes of the Hohenzollerns began to improve. With the ending of the Thirty Years' War in 1648, the Elector had the opportunity to step forward as the leading champion of north German Protestantism. Not all his claims were recognized, but the peacemakers of Westphalia allowed him to absorb valuable territories in the central German Plain and along the shores of the Baltic. Thus, although his lands were ravaged by the war, Frederick William was able to lay the foundations of a modern state. It was

PREVIOUS PAGES Frederick III, grandfather of Frederick the Great, crowns himself King Frederick I of Prussia.

12

his ambition to weld the divided portions of his realm into a single
unity centred on Berlin and preserved from envious neighbours by
a formidable standing army. Outwardly he was successful, winning for a small state of a million and a half people a militaristic
reputation far beyond its natural resources. A sycophantic Court
poet once lauded him as 'the Great Elector' and the honorific title
has survived the scrutiny of later historians. Yet it is significant
that in his final testament Frederick William sought to divide his
lands between the sons of his two marriages, thereby tacitly

Friedrich Wilhelm I.
König in Preussen.
geb. 1688. gest. 1740.

LEFT Frederick William I of Prussia, Frederick's brutal and boorish father.
ABOVE The young Frederick with his sister Wilhelmina in the park.
Wilhelmina later became his greatest friend.

acknowledging a doubt over the wisdom of maintaining under a single ruler possessions on the Baltic, in central Germany and on the lower Rhine. Fortunately for Prussia, this proposal was ignored by the Great Elector's eldest son, whose prime task in diplomacy was to secure recognition from the Emperor Leopold in Vienna of his right to be styled Prussia's king. It was this concession (technically limited to the Hohenzollern lands outside the confines of the Empire) which prompted the celebrations at Königsberg in January 1701.

Frederick I was not a remarkable ruler. Indeed, no subsequent event in his reign was so impressive as his coronation. The Great Elector taxed his subjects severely in order to create the Prussian army, but at least he also increased the real wealth of his peoples by developing trade and industry. His son maintained the high level of taxation, but allocated most of the revenue to the royal household in order to pay for new palaces in Berlin and other luxuries. Culturally Prussia benefited from Frederick I's extravagance – and even more from the good taste of his Queen, Sophia Charlotte of Hanover, a sister of the English King George I. But the royal couple's partiality for magnificent buildings and elegant furniture was not shared by their son, Crown Prince Frederick William, nor by the honest, beer-swilling, pipe-puffing army commanders who kept the Crown Prince company in his leisure hours. To these veterans of Blenheim, Oudenarde and Malplaquet (where Frederick William had himself come under fire) there was something ridiculous, perhaps even unmanly, in the King's concern with the outward attributes of royal dignity. The Crown Prince had no pretensions towards gentility. His circle was narrowly philistine, despising and distrusting the many Germans, both inside and outside Prussia, who looked to Paris and Versailles as models for the art of living. Frederick William was a good son, scrupulously loyal and obedient; he even wore a Spanish-style perruque so long as his father believed the fashion to be essential for Court dress. But when, in February 1713, he succeeded to the throne, he at once set about ridding his realm of foreign affectation – and, at the same time, freeing his exchequer from its burden of accumulated debts. Frederick I had spent some five million thalers on his coronation at Königsberg: twelve years later Frederick William I cut expenditure for his own coronation ceremonies down to a frugally precise 2,547 thalers. The contrast between these figures is an apt commentary on the difference between Prussia's first two kings.

OPPOSITE Frederick's grandmother, Sophia Charlotte, the sister of George I of England. Prussia benefited enormously from the good taste she showed in the decoration of magnificent palaces.

When Frederick I died, his eldest grandson was a mere thirteen months old. Young Frederick could not, therefore, remember in later years any other ruler of Prussia than his father. His childhood coincided with the period in which, to use his own phrase, Frederick William was hoping to turn Berlin from 'the Athens of the North . . . into its Sparta'. The King, with his hatred of everything French, was determined that his son should be trained as a good new recruit for the Prussian army rather than become yet another princely imitator of Gallic ways. 'Fritz' was woken each morning by the discharge of blank shot from a cannon beneath his window; and, before he was even old enough to be dressed in boys' clothing, he was given a full-sized drum to strap around his waist and beat up and down the corridors of the palace. By the age of five he knew all fifty-four movements of the Prussian Drill Code. A year later, in grenadier's uniform, he had his own company of child cadets, whom he marched to church each Sunday; on one memorable occasion he paraded them for inspection by the visiting Tsar, Peter the Great. Before his eighth birthday the Crown Prince possessed a miniature arsenal of his own, a collection of working models which enabled him to familiarize himself with every weapon of war. There was nothing wrong with Fritz's military education, except perhaps its precocity.

It was far harder for Frederick William to have the boy's mind shaped as he desired. At first he entrusted Fritz to Madame de Roucolle, a Huguenot refugee who had been the King's own governess thirty years previously. She was, he knew, a God-fearing Calvinist who abhorred the dandified fashions of her native land. But in 1719 Frederick William became concerned about his health: he began to suffer from acute stomach pains and it seemed, for a time, as if Fritz might succeed to the throne while still a child. At once the King resolved to institute a more rigorous system of instruction. He appointed the sixty-year-old General von Finckenstein as the boy's governor, with another distinguished soldier, Colonel von Kalkstein, as Finckenstein's deputy. Formal tuition was left to a thirty-four-year-old Huguenot officer, Jacques Duhan, who had attracted the King's attention by his exemplary courage in the wars. To safeguard Fritz from dangerous doctrines, the three men were given an elaborate directive which regulated the boy's daily routine and listed the King's idiosyncratic taboos (no Latin, no ancient history, no mention of the doctrine of predestination). They were told when he should rise, when he should wash and dress, even when he should pray. There could be no unsoldierly moments of leisure although the King conceded that after five in the afternoon 'Fritz shall . . . divert himself in the open air (and never in his room) and then do whatever he wishes, so long as it is not against the will of God'.

At first the system seemed to work well enough. Fritz dutifully wrote for his father an essay on 'The Life-Style of a Prince of High Birth': it was a portrait of a good soldier, frugal in his habits and pious in his beliefs. The King commended his son publicly, but even he had doubts. 'When you grow older', he asked, 'won't you behave like everyone else in your station of life? Won't you eat and drink too much, swear and scold, grow callous and go after

Frederick's mother, Sophia Dorothea, a sister of George II of England, and therefore both the niece and daughter-in-law of Frederick's grandmother. A somewhat plain and weak woman, she could not shield her son from the rages of his father, but she did what she could to encourage his interest in the arts.

19

whores?' 'No, Papa', was the prim response, 'I shall hold fast to the Ten Commandments.'

It was, of course, too good to be true. No lad of spirit could develop his mind, or allow his natural instincts to mature, under such a rigidly austere code of behaviour as his father devised. Young Frederick was remarkably intelligent, Duhan was an excellent teacher, and there were enough books collected in his grandfather's reign for the Crown Prince to receive a first-rate education; but inevitably the chief effect of the King's instructions was to make his son secretive, shy and reserved. Frederick William began to suspect the Crown Prince's honesty and intentions. 'What is going on in that little head?' the King complained pathetically when Fritz was twelve years old, 'I know he does not think as I do.' Neither Finckenstein nor Kalkstein could give an answer, and Duhan was far too sensible to say a word. For the next ten years father and son were separated by a wall of incomprehension and antipathy.

Thomas Carlyle, writing the first of his massive volumes on Frederick the Great in the early 1840s, painted a horrifying picture of a young prince terrorized by a lunatic father who was jealous of his gifted son's superior intellect. At times Carlyle's passionate sympathy with his hero led him to accept uncritically wild stories of the home life of the Hohenzollerns which a less committed biographer might reasonably have treated with reserve. Yet there is no doubt that Carlyle's account of Frederick's humiliations captures the brutality of this terrible phase of his life. Frequently Frederick William was himself in pain from inflammation of the kidneys or from gout, and at such times he did not care who was present when he abused his son. If he thought the heir to the throne was 'a cringing coward' or 'a slovenly bookworm' he said so outright, often belabouring Frederick with the rattan cane he invariably carried with him. The King's outbursts are recorded in the despatches of diplomats at Court as well as in the memoirs of those who were later to help Frederick raise Prussia's status in Europe. We read of Frederick William's anger over his son's alleged effeminacy, of his contempt for a boy who wore gloves while hunting in the deep frosts of winter and leaped from the saddle of a bolting horse. And there were other lapses of grace, all treated with equal gravity: the day on which Frederick settled down to read a novel in a thicket rather than stalk deer; the discovery that he preferred to eat with a silver fork of three prongs rather than with the standard two pronged metal fork favoured by

OPPOSITE Frederick's enthusiasm for military affairs began at an early age. Here he wears the uniform of the Grenadier Cadets, of whom he was the nominal commander.

21

the King's drinking cronies; and the absurd occasion when Frederick William swished his rattan in uncontrollable rage on finding the boy had talked his tutors into teaching him some Latin. At fourteen, wrote one foreign observer, the Crown Prince looked so weary that 'despite his youth, he seems as old and walks as stiffly as though he had already participated in several campaigns'.

It would, however, be a mistake to imagine Frederick's adolescence as a protracted period of perpetual persecution. Frederick William was a diligent ruler, often journeying on tours of inspection through his scattered territories; and, though he sometimes insisted that his son should accompany him, he was reluctant to take the boy away from his studies. At such times Frederick delighted in the companionship of his mother, Sophia Dorothea, a sister of George II of England. Although not so refined or gifted as her mother-in-law (and aunt) Sophia Charlotte, the Queen succeeded in appearing as a patron of the arts without understanding them, and she encouraged the aesthetic traits in Frederick's character. She was far too frightened of her husband ever to make a stand on behalf of Frederick or any other of her ten surviving children, but her apartments were a convenient place of refuge into which her eldest son was thankful to escape. They were also, according to the ambassadors, the only comfortable rooms in the palace.

Throughout this difficult phase of his life Frederick found in his eldest sister, Wilhelmina, a more reliable ally than his mother. Wilhelmina, his one close friend in childhood, was slightly more than two years his senior. She shared her brother's liking for music and the arts – for all those 'comedies, operas, ballets, masquerades and tournaments' which their father roundly condemned as 'godless things increasing the kingdom of the Devil'. Occasionally Frederick and Wilhelmina seem deliberately to have provoked the unfortunate King, either by displaying an interest in forbidden subjects or by seeking to score verbal points off him in argument, and then, as soon as they had worked him into a violent temper, they would flee rapidly anywhere beyond the range of his stick. One wonders if these curious diversions were mere adolescent mischief or whether there was anything more subtle in the children's minds, for there was always a possibility that a man of Frederick William's build – short and corpulent with pendant cheeks flushed crimson and a squat neck overflowing his collar – would fall dead from apoplexy during one of these fits of rage.

Had he done so, Frederick was ready for the succession: he

22

amazed both the British and the French envoys when his father was critically ill in 1726 by the calm way in which he calculated the prospects of a change of ruler and by the assurance with which he outlined his programme of action. His mind was as cold and clear as the steel-like gaze of those staggeringly alert blue eyes. It was odd that his father should insist that Frederick was a 'dreamy poet and piper' when it was evident to anyone who talked seriously to him that the Crown Prince possessed a rapier sharpness of intellect and knew well enough where he was going.

Yet, as Frederick reached manhood, it became increasingly clear that his objectives did not coincide with those of his father. Despite his extraordinary temperament, Frederick William was one of the most energetic and constructive rulers in Prussia's history, as both his eldest son and eldest daughter acknowledged in later years. A series of administrative reforms in 1722–3 effectively centralized authority throughout the country in the hands of the monarch, while careful royal husbandry improved the agrarian economy and stimulated profitable industries. These, however, were not measures to thrill the imagination of the young: one did not appreciate bureaucratic achievements if one was convinced that the head bureaucrat himself was a ridiculous and unlettered bumbler, prematurely cantankerous. It was remarkable that Frederick William succeeded in building up his army so that it became the most powerful within Germany – and all this without making the country bankrupt. But Frederick could see no reason why, with such troops at his disposal, the King wished to play second fiddle to the Habsburgs in Vienna rather than challenge them for the effective leadership of the German states. Could it be that Frederick William wanted a powerful army as a toy, something to parade across his territories with that delight which he always found in drilling his regiment of giant Potsdam Grenadiers? Frederick William was indeed too passionately attached to his army to risk its destruction in a dangerous gamble, but it is also arguable that he wished Prussia to be militarily impressive as a guarantee of keeping peace within Germany, and thereby ensuring cohesion between his divided territories. This was a sophisticated policy which only a ruler of experience and long memory would understand.

The Crown Prince's views on foreign affairs were simpler, and reflected the slightly muddled prejudices of his mother. Frederick wanted to work closely with England-Hanover so as to provide a third force in the centre of the continent, independent both of

Austria and France. There was more behind this proposal than conventional diplomacy. The Queen, proud of her English dynastic connections, had long favoured a double marriage link between Berlin and London: Wilhelmina, she hoped, would marry George II's son and become Princess of Wales, while Frederick would take George's second daughter, Amelia, as his wife. Both Wilhelmina and Frederick were delighted at the marriage project. Frederick William, on the other hand, though inclined to the idea in 1725, changed his policy and his mind a few months later and refused to hear anything more of it. He disliked George II intensely, having quarrelled with him at Hanover in childhood and never felt inclined for a cousinly reconciliation, and he spoke gloomily of the risk that some Anglo-Hanoverian Crown Princess would foment intrigues in his capital, for he was convinced any girl brought up at the English Court would wish to play politics. Moreover, being the son of one Hanoverian princess and the husband of another, he felt it would be too much if he became father-in-law of a third female member of the Guelph family. Hopefully he suggested that Wilhelmina might be packed off to London if there was a prospect she would one day be England's Queen: George II was unresponsive.

His father's veto of an English marriage alienated Frederick still further. He became increasingly friendly with successive English envoys to Berlin, even receiving gifts of money from his royal uncle in order to pay off the debts he was accumulating through his secret purchase of forbidden luxuries. This was a dangerous development: it made Frederick virtually an English pensionary. The fact that Grumbkow, Frederick William's chief minister, was widely suspected of being in Austrian pay only complicated the situation, for if the latent power struggle at Court between the Habsburg faction and the Anglo-Hanoverian faction came into the open, the heir to the throne would be compromised, and Grumbkow was far too ruthless to spare Frederick embarrassment.

Fortunately, in the opening months of 1728, a happy diversion provided a chance of reconciliation between father and son. Frederick William was invited to make a month-long state visit to Dresden by the Elector of Saxony, Augustus II, who urged the King to bring the young Crown Prince with him. Rather surprisingly, Frederick William accepted the invitation and encouraged Frederick to fit himself out in fashionable clothes. Augustus was too important a figure politically to be refused: as well as ruling Saxony, he had been elective King of Poland for the past thirty

years and therefore controlled the broad Vistulan corridor across which Frederick William had to journey every time he travelled from Berlin to Königsberg. Moreover, there is no doubt that he was curious to see Dresden in all its glorious decadence.

It is hard to imagine a greater contrast than the austere Court of Berlin and the exquisitely beautiful palaces of Dresden, nor indeed between the puritanical Frederick William and the sensual, hedonistic giant Augustus 'the Strong'. To have fathered almost as many bastards as there were days in the year and then to have

During the eighteenth century, war became an art, something to be studied in great detail. This early print depicts such studies. It took a Frederick to upset the theories.

25

Frederick's brothers depicted together. *From left to right* Frederick, Ferdinand, Augustus William and Henry.

taken one of his illegitimate daughters as a favourite mistress showed exotic eccentricity even in the eighteenth century, and Frederick William could never approve of his brother sovereign's way of life. But he enjoyed himself mightily, his prurience titillated by what he saw. 'I am thankful to say that I left as pure as when I came', the King declared later. It was a claim his son could not make. For young Frederick the visit to Saxony surpassed all expectation. He was treated with respect, permitted to go openly to

26

the theatre and the opera, allowed to talk philosophy around the dinner-table, welcomed to balls and banquets, and abetted when he wished to escape parental vigilance and succumb to the natural temptations of his environment. 'Fritz, Fritz, I am afraid you like it here all too much', his father lamented. Dresden was not the best finishing school for a Prince of Hohenzollern.

For the rest of the year 1728 life seemed almost unbearable for Frederick. His father returned from Saxony not to Berlin or Potsdam but to a small and dismal hunting-lodge, Wusterhausen, twenty miles south-east of the capital. Frederick had always hated the place, with its dank marshes, eagles tethered to the draw-bridge, and the invariable routine of hunting, smoking and drinking, but after Dresden he found Wusterhausen so depressing that, as Wilhelmina perceived, his spirit was almost broken. Once more their father began hitting him with his rattan and kicking him in public, and here there was nowhere for him to seek refuge except a bleak cell-like room above the moat. From there, on 11 September, he sent a wretchedly miserable note to the 'dear Papa, whom for some time past I have been unable to nerve myself to visit', begging him 'to be gracious . . . and discard the cruel hatred I have had sufficient occasion to observe in all his treatment of me'. The only answer he received was a thunderous denunciation of 'a self-willed young man . . . so effeminate . . . that he can neither ride nor shoot . . . and who wears his hair long and foolishly curled'. To emphasize the estrangement of father and son, Frederick William's reply was written in the third person.

Frederick, however, was genuinely ill; the doctors feared he was wasting away with consumption. On his eventual return to Berlin he seemed so near death that the King was momentarily filled with remorse, and swore that if he recovered his health the boy should enjoy a little more recreation, provided of course he was never left on his own. When at last he was convalescent, Frederick William went on one of his tours to East Prussia and in his absence Fritz, with his mother's connivance, was able to ignore most of the restraints imposed upon him. It was at this time that he formed an intimate friendship with Hans von Katte, son of the commanding general at Königsberg and nephew to George I's singularly plain mistress, the Duchess of Kendal. Young Katte, a lieutenant in the Royal Guard, was a good-looking aesthete, with a taste for music and French literature, a welcome companion for both Frederick and Wilhelmina. There was never any hope that he would win his sovereign's approbation.

27

Dresden

A courtyard of the palace of the Electors of Saxony. It was in this city that Frederick discovered manhood – and the freedom that accompanied it.

ABOVE The fountain of the palace.
LEFT and RIGHT Two statues from the courtyard, traditionally two of the mistresses of Augustus the Strong.

With the coming of the winter of 1729-30, Frederick William had forgotten his good intentions (in so far as they ever existed) and he was once more baiting Frederick unmercifully. The Crown Prince decided he could not stand a life of public insult any longer. Significantly the King himself at one time taunted him for having calmly accepted harsh treatment, insisting that he personally would have committed suicide or run away rather than submit to such indignities. With Frederick dead, the succession would pass to the King's favourite son, Augustus William, and the Crown Prince had no intention of obliging his father and brother by killing himself. But flight from the country was a different matter. The thought of escape had long attracted him. He talked it over with Katte and another friend, Lieutenant Keith; he let Wilhelmina see him in one of the disguises he planned to wear, and she did her best to dissuade him from any act of folly. At last he took into his confidence a personal envoy from George II, who made it clear that a fugitive heir to the Prussian throne would prove far too embarrassing a guest for his English relatives to protect. Only the young madcaps, Katte and Keith, encouraged him – and they were soon sent away from Berlin to their regiments. Neither of them was as discreet as good sense demanded.

The crisis came in July 1730. It began with an angry scene in which Frederick William finally put an end to the Anglo-Hanoverian marriage project. A few days later he was due to leave Potsdam for a grand progress through the German states, visiting Nuremberg, Augsburg and Stuttgart and then down the Main and the Rhine to his own western lands along the frontier with the Netherlands. He had not intended to take Frederick with him, but at the last moment he changed his mind. Two colonels were ordered by the King to accompany the heir to the throne as equerries, and never once to let him out of their sight. It is hard to escape the feeling that either the King, or one of his close advisers, was deliberately tempting Frederick to make a fool of himself, discrediting him so that he would renounce his future rights to the crown. Grumbkow and the pro-Austrian faction had much to gain and nothing to lose by the disgrace of a Prince who had made himself so agreeable to the English and the French.

What followed was a stupid escapade, tragic in its consequences for more than one family. On the night of 3 August the royal cavalcade halted at the small village of Steinfurt, south of Heidelberg and little more than forty miles from the French border. Frederick planned to set out soon after two o'clock next morning,

One of the tobacco evenings in which Frederick's father loved to indulge, and which Frederick loathed.

slipping away while his companions were still asleep and then heading for the Rhine. He relied, for assistance, on Lieutenant Keith's younger brother, a page in the King's suite, who would saddle a couple of horses for him and ride with him to the frontier. All went wrong. The Crown Prince's guardians awoke, found him waiting for the horses, and escorted him firmly back to his carriage; but they said nothing next morning to the King. It was, however, too much for the page's nerves. The wretched lad decided to seek out Frederick William after his return from the morning service (for it was a Sunday), tell his master all he knew and implore his mercy. For the moment, the King took no action apart from reprimanding his son's guardians for not informing him of what had happened in the small hours. But on Monday the storm broke in earnest. That day Frederick William reached Frankfurt-on-Main: there he received a misdirected letter, originating from Katte and intended for Frederick, which seemed to prove that the Prince planned to settle abroad and conspire against his father with the help of his friends. Frederick was interrogated and physically assaulted by the King, who ordered him to be placed in custody on a charge of desertion and to be conveyed, under escort, to the fortress of Küstrin in south-eastern Prussia. Katte, having ignored ample warnings of disaster through sheer pigheadedness, was arrested in Berlin on 16 August; the elder of the Keith brothers escaped to England; the younger was placed under detention in Wesel, the Hohenzollern outpost on the Rhine.

Katte was subjected to five interrogations and threatened with torture. Frederick himself was kept in solitary confinement for a fortnight and then handed a questionnaire which assumed him guilty and was clearly intended to frighten him into renouncing the succession under fear of life imprisonment or death. At the end of October a court-martial, convened under considerable royal pressure, found Katte guilty of conspiring with Frederick to desert from the army and of intriguing with foreign envoys; it recommended that he should be imprisoned for life. The officers of the court-martial insisted, however, that they were not competent to try the Crown Prince, as Frederick William demanded. There was considerable sympathy for Frederick in Berlin, and even more in the other courts of Germany, and no member of the Prussian ruling class wanted to blacken his own reputation by condoning an act of injustice towards the titular heir to the throne.

By now, however, Frederick William himself was hardly a sane man. He ordered vengeance to be taken on all of Frederick's friends.

OPPOSITE The foolish and headstrong Hans Hermann von Katte, who was to lose his head for abetting Frederick's attempted escape from his father.

33

ABOVE A painting by Frederick William of himself (in the centre), with servants and grenadiers.

RIGHT Frederick's father with the dissolute Augustus the Strong of Saxony, during the visit to Dresden. Augustus was soon to drink himself to death.

'The scum Wilhelmina', as he called his daughter, was imprisoned in her room and threatened with execution. Three young officers in Frederick's circle were cashiered and incarcerated in Spandau. So too was Dorothea Ritter, a sixteen-year-old girl with a talent for music, who was also condemned to be whipped in front of her father's house and at every street corner in Potsdam for having received presents from Frederick as a reward for accompanying him on the lute in happier days. After such savagery, there was little hope for Katte. When the young lieutenant's father sent an appeal for clemency to the King, Frederick William wrote in reply: 'Your son is a scoundrel, so is mine – and so what can we poor fathers do?'

The King was determined that Katte must die, irrespective of the court-martial verdict. At five o'clock in the morning of 6 November, Frederick was woken from his sleep and told that Katte had arrived in Küstrin, where he would be executed in two hours' time. On his father's orders, the Prince was taken to a window so that he might witness the beheading of his friend, a means – wrote Frederick William – 'of softening Fritz's hardened heart'. But in this expectation, at least, the King was thwarted. As Katte knelt on the block in the courtyard, his royal companion, pinioned to the window above, fainted into merciful unconsciousness and did not see the sabre fall.

OPPOSITE Katte's execution: a nineteenth-century view of the farewell between him and Frederick a few moments before Frederick fainted.

37

2
Cultivating Tranquillity

FREDERICK HAD NEVER ANTICIPATED his father would insist on Katte's execution, still less that such a terrible sentence would be carried out beneath his own window. The shock of the nightmare events of that grey November morning unnerved him; he knew it was his own desire to escape from Prussia which had led to Katte's disgrace; momentarily he believed he deserved a similar fate and that his father would insist that he, too, should pay the penalty of folly. But there were limits to Frederick William's awful sense of Calvinistic discipline. With Katte's death, his wrath seemed dissipated. The chaplain at Küstrin reported that the Prince was praying for God's mercy and the King's pardon; and from Vienna Charles VI, who as Emperor had a duty to intervene if the life of an heir to an Electorate were threatened, urged the Prussian King to show clemency. Hence within a fortnight of Katte's execution, Frederick William decided that, provided his son renewed his oath of allegiance, he might be released from custody. On 19 November Frederick pledged his loyalty, 'loudly and clearly' as the King demanded, and was handed back his sword.

He was not, however, as yet re-instated in the army. Frederick William ordered him to remain at Küstrin and gave instructions he should be found employment as a minor civil servant in the local departmental council of war and agriculture. The Crown Prince was to be accorded no privileges: he could not leave the confines of the small town; he was forbidden to entertain guests, listen to secular music, write any letters except to his parents or read any books apart from the Bible, a hymnal and a study of Christianity. Each Sunday, Frederick, whom his father believed to be tainted with Katte's alleged atheism, was to attend divine service twice in the morning and once in the evening. There is no evidence that this experience of penitential discipline made Frederick any more inclined to accept the traditional faith of his ancestors.

In practice, his enforced exile at Küstrin was less oppressive than the tone of these restrictions suggests, for Frederick was soon able to evade most of them. A sympathetic guard even reported to a friend that the Prince was delighting his colleagues on the council with his humour and that he was 'as happy as a chaffinch'. By good fortune the King entrusted Frederick's introduction to civil administration to Christoph Hille, an intelligent official who was also a natural teacher. Hille was convinced good government required a detailed understanding of the petty problems of the domestic economy rather than the ability to formulate broad

PREVIOUS PAGES Merry-making at Rheinsberg: on the left is Frederick's great friend Jordan, while opposite him is Baron Keyserlingk.

40

A contemporary picture of
Frederick learning the
practical crafts of the land –
a duty demanded by his
father but one he found
interesting.

policies from the loftiest of motives. He was a blunt, hard-working
commoner with a healthy disrespect for rank but a willingness to
explain to his royal charge all the complexities of local administration, provided the Prince would listen, and though Frederick often
complained the hours at Küstrin passed slowly, he found Hille's
unusual approach to public affairs interesting.

The King had written that 'Director Hille must show him the
true value of a well-ordered household, letting him see for himself
how a peasant earns a thaler', and this task Hille dutifully performed. But he was also told to explain to the Prince 'all sorts of
business connected with the working of a council'. Thus it was
that Frederick, for the first time in his life, became aware of difficulties in the linen industry, of the varying yields on the Crown
estates from livestock and brewing, and, above all, of the envy and
suspicion felt by small manufacturers towards their long-estab-
lished rivals in Austrian Silesia. He began to see the importance of
a settled trading policy. More and more he sensed the economic
disadvantages imposed on Brandenburg–Prussia by the fragmenta-

41

tion of her territories. Within eleven weeks of beginning work at Hille's side, he wrote a remarkable letter to his trusted confidant, Karl von Natzmer, in which he spoke of the kingdom's need to absorb Swedish-held Lower Pomerania and the Polish lands which cut off East Prussia from Brandenburg. Under Hille's guidance he was discovering for himself a realistic approach to the map of Europe very different from anything he gathered from more formal tutors in earlier years.

'My spell in the galleys', as Frederick later called his days at Küstrin, also modified his attitude towards his father. He was unwilling to forgive Frederick William for his brutality, nor was he

sincere in humbling himself when the King came to Küstrin, but, for the first time, the Prince began to respect Frederick William's shrewdness over domestic affairs, and to understand the care he gave to routine matters of trade and administration. In August 1731, on the King's birthday, it seemed for a moment as if there might be a reconciliation for, when father and son met, each shed tears at the memory of all that happened twelve months before. But Frederick William, too, could neither forget nor forgive. He would not trust his eldest son and daughter. With minimum consideration for Wilhelmina's feelings, he found her a convenient husband, the dull and earnest Prince of Bayreuth, and a few months

A view of the grim fortress of Küstrin where Katte was beheaded, and where Frederick was forced to remain in exile.

43

later he sent Grumbkow to inform Frederick that he also must marry. The Prince was perfectly willing to take a wife: he explained that, if she could not be an English princess, then he had no objection to the Emperor's daughter, Maria Theresa. But his father allowed him no choice. Frederick would marry, not the Emperor's daughter (heiress-designate to the Habsburg lands) but the Empress's niece, Elizabeth-Christine of Brunswick, a pudding of a girl, devoid of charm and suitors.

Frederick was made angry and depressed by this latest instance of his father's enmity. Reluctantly he agreed, in March 1732, to

Frederick's marriage to Elizabeth-Christine of Brunswick–Brandenburg on 12 June 1733.

a formal betrothal; he was assured he would receive a sufficient income to maintain an establishment of his own and that he would be permitted to resume a military career. Even so, fifteen months elapsed between the betrothal ceremony and the wedding. Briefly, in the early weeks of 1733, it seemed as if a shift of Prussian policy might allow Frederick to gain the English marriage he had so long sought; but soon the necessities of German politics again pointed to a Brunswick–Brandenburg connection, and on 12 June Frederick and Elizabeth-Christine were married, the Crown Prince even acting out the part of a happy bridegroom so long as he was

A flattering portrait of Frederick's wife: in reality she was plump, plain and ill-educated, and though she loved her husband, he could never forgive her for these faults.

45

Bernardo Bellotto genannt
Canaletto Pinx

PREVIOUS PAGES Dresden, the capital of Saxony, where Frederick discovered that life was not just books and marching. A painting by Canaletto.

in his father's presence. Yet he could not overcome his antipathy towards the unfortunate girl. Privately he complained that she was not only unattractive, but maladroit and ill-educated as well. After one night in the bridal chamber he wrote to his sister Wilhelmina, 'Thank God that is over.' Elizabeth-Christine, sadly, had genuinely fallen in love with Frederick; and she continued to idolize him for the remainder of his life. At best her loyalty won from him a glacial respect.

Frederick William, however, kept his word. Frederick was appointed Colonel of a grenadier regiment and assigned a residence at Neuruppin, a small garrison town forty miles north of Berlin. His wife amused herself, in his absence, at a château which the King presented to her on the outskirts of the capital. Neuruppin was as much a cultural desert as Küstrin, and the King took care to see that the Prince's regimental officers did not come from the sophisticated aristocratic families; but Frederick's attention to his military duties mollified his father, who agreed he should purchase an estate at Rheinsberg (some fifteen miles from Neuruppin) and refurbish the tumbledown medieval castle so as to make it an elegant country mansion, a home fit for a Crown Prince and his consort. A transformation on this scale could not, however, be hurried, and it was only in the summer of 1736 that Frederick and Elizabeth-Christine were able to take up residence at Rheinsberg. Before then, Frederick was unexpectedly given opportunities to see active service in the field and to broaden his acquaintance with the German lands to the west and the east of Brandenburg.

The campaign of 1734 was an unimpressive affair, confused in purpose and execution. At the height of the previous summer, Augustus the Strong of Saxony had confounded his awed physicians by at last drinking himself to death. There was no difficulty over the succession to his Saxon title: his son, Augustus III, became Elector. But the Polish nobility, under French pressure, elected as King one of their own number, Stanislas Lesczynski, who was father-in-law of Louis XV. None of Poland's neighbours wished to see the country fall under the influence of France. The Emperor Charles VI supported the claims of Augustus III to rule in Warsaw as well as in Dresden. So too did the Russians, who invaded Poland and drove out Stanislas while the Austrians prepared to take care of the French. Technically Brandenburg–Prussia remained neutral but Frederick William wished to have a voice in the future of Poland and offered the Emperor an expeditionary force. Charles VI, deciding that the issue must be settled on France's

48

frontiers rather than on the Polish plains, gave the legendary Prince Eugene command of the Imperial Army in the Rhineland and accepted from Frederick William a contingent of ten thousand men. Attached to them, at his own insistent request, was Crown Prince Frederick.

To serve under the veteran hero of Oudenarde and Malplaquet seemed an honour in itself, and Frederick was pleased his father had given him permission to leave Neuruppin for the Rhineland. At seventy-one, however, Prince Eugene was little more than a

Augustus III of Poland, son of Augustus the Strong: his controversial succession to the throne was responsible for the first war Frederick saw.

name from a glorious past. The campaign gave Frederick his baptism of fire, French cannon raking a wood outside Philippsburg as he was riding by on reconnaissance, but otherwise the experience was far from memorable. He watched the Imperial Army observing the classical precepts of siege warfare and was not impressed. Nor, indeed, was Frederick William who decided to keep an eye on his troops (and, incidentally, on his son) and insisted on spending a damp month under canvas. It seemed that autumn as if the rain would never stop: it put an end to Prince Eugene's campaign and it almost put an end to Frederick William, too. For the King's obstinacy overstrained his health. He collapsed with what appears to have been pneumonia and was borne slowly back to Potsdam. The physicians told Frederick his father had, at best, another fortnight of life ahead of him. The Crown Prince shed dutiful tears of remorse, and hurried back to the capital.

But incredibly, Frederick William rallied. That Christmas the Prussian Court did indeed observe mourning. It was, however, a sign of respect for Frederick's departed father-in-law and not his father who, at the time, was enjoying a more rancorous season of peace and ill-will than for several years past. Frederick still had to contend with the King's baiting tongue, even if he was now relieved from the danger of physical assault. Once again he felt cheated by the physicians, and his sense of filial duty was severely taxed. 'The Duke of Brunswick', he declared to his sister, 'being a man of honour, has had the decency to die – unlike someone else.'

When spring came, the Crown Prince asked permission to return to the Rhineland ready for the next campaign against the French. His father, however, insisted he should remain at Neuruppin with his regiment. There were, he added mysteriously, 'good reasons' why he wished him to stay in Brandenburg, although when Frederick tried to find out what these reasons were, his father merely lost his temper. At the time Frederick assumed his father's veto was proof of continued doubt over his son's loyalty. This may well have been the case: the Prince barely succeeded in hiding his admiration for French culture which, to a man of Frederick William's limited intellectual interests, seemed tantamount to admiring the King of France and all his ministers too. But there may also have been a sound political reason. To Frederick William, the 'War of the Polish Succession' seemed to have lost any purpose it had ever possessed. By now it was clear that Emperor Charles VI wished to negotiate a settlement with Louis XV and that, whatever

50

might be decided elsewhere, the Polish question would be resolved in favour of the rulers of Saxony rather than of Stanislas Lesczynski. For the moment, this suited Prussia well enough: an absentee king was preferable to a Polish nobleman on the throne. But Frederick William was willing to give hospitality to the unfortunate Stanislas when he felt betrayed by his earlier patrons. With a gesture of independence which startled the Emperor, Frederick William encouraged the Crown Prince to visit Königsberg in the summer of 1735 and entertain the exiled Pole in the royal castle. It was better for a future King of Prussia to acquire a practical knowledge of Polish affairs than to waste another wet summer under canvas in the Rhineland.

There were, of course, other reasons for sending Frederick to East Prussia. The whole area had been devastated by the plague shortly before Frederick William's accession, more than a third of the able-bodied population perishing in the years 1709-11, and the King had always given great attention to rehabilitating this distant marchland. Frederick was much impressed by the work of Huguenot refugees in the towns and by the effectiveness of his father's reforms in the countryside, especially to the immediate south and west of Königsberg where famine had followed the terrible epidemic. As at other moments when he felt matters deeply he affected a boorish cynicism: 'Were you only here', he wrote to one of his rakish friends, 'I could offer you a choice between the prettiest Lithuanian girls and the best mares in the royal stud, for there is no more difference between a daughter of these parts and a mare than there is between cattle and cattle.' But in reality he was stirred by the prospects of colonization in the East and he returned to Berlin with a new respect for what Frederick William had achieved by his attention to the dreary routine of administrative detail. As Frederick himself admitted, he was never so well-disposed towards his father as when they were far apart.

The next four years were as happy as any in Frederick's life. His regimental commitments in Neuruppin were few, and apart from occasional duty visits to Potsdam or the hated Wusterhausen, he spent almost every day at Rheinsberg, delighting in the consciously cultured Court he was creating amid the marshland and lakes of the lower Havel. Crown Princess Elizabeth-Christine, too, liked Rheinsberg and made a pathetic attempt to please her husband by improving her mind through the study of ancient philosophy, with her chaplain as a tutor. But Frederick, who had an unattractive habit of humiliating anyone openly showing him affection, mocked

51

her laborious efforts. After a few months the unfortunate Elizabeth-Christine began to find diversions of her own. They were always virtuous and spontaneously natural and yet, to her husband, they appeared inexcusably commonplace. He did not object to her presence at his dinner-table, sometimes he was even seen walking or riding with her, and he was generally polite to her ladies-in-waiting, provided that – like everyone at Rheinsberg except the menials – they conversed in French. But at heart he favoured solely masculine companionship. He liked to sit late at night talking to his old friend Baron von Keyserlingk, or exchanging ideas with the rich and well-read Huguenot pastor Charles Etienne

A view across the river of Rheinsberg, a medieval castle which Frederick bought and restored, and where he spent some of the happiest hours of his life.

52

Jordan, who acted as the Prince's secretary; and he was especially attached to another French émigré, the Baron de la Motte Fouqué, who had befriended him first at Küstrin. The management of the household at Rheinsberg was left to the Prince's former valet Michael Fredersdorf, a private soldier who was such a good flautist that Frederick insisted on treating him as a close friend. From the tone of their letters it would seem as if this unusual relationship of master and servant meant more to the Prince than the intimacy of any other man or woman.

Yet although Frederick intended Rheinsberg to be a cheerful place where at last he might relax and enjoy himself, he imposed

Baron von Keyserlingk, a pleasure-hunting but intellectual man, with whom Frederick spent many late nights in discussion.

upon his Court a curiously austere code of behaviour: we read, in the memoirs, of hearty pranks but not of excessive drunkenness or nights of debauchery as in so many similar societies on the continent at this time. Rheinsberg had a unique purpose in his scheme of existence: it was a country house where he could mirror his personal tastes, but it was also the centre of a community of his own choosing, somewhere for him to pursue the 'Enlightenment Ideal' of a life based upon reason, good talk and letters. His father's persecution had crippled the development of Frederick's intellectual faculties; he knew a little about many subjects but had studied none systematically. Hence his thought, like the verse he wrote, was essentially ill-blended, fragmentary and second-hand. He hoped Rheinsberg would serve him as a university as much as a home. It was easy enough to be a dilettante tasting the arts with an exquisitely refined palate; that had been the fashion of his grandmother and, less successfully, of his mother, too. But Frederick was not content to be a patron: he wished to organize his reading and mental relaxation, consciously training himself as a person and a ruler. He also believed that at Rheinsberg he would be able to observe mankind in the abstract with philosophic detachment and at peace with himself. Other princes might have seen more of the world but there could be none among his contemporaries who had read so deeply. When his architect and friend Baron von Knobelsdorff, rebuilt the front façade of Rheinsberg he inserted in the stonework a Latin dedication: *Frederico tranquillitatem colenti*, 'To Frederick, the cultivator of tranquillity.' It was an apt inscription for an eighteenth-century man of letters – though not perhaps for the soldier who was to win Rossbach and Leuthen and bring the avenging Russian and Austrian armies down on Berlin.

All this, however, lay far in the future in that first autumn he spent at Rheinsberg. For the moment he was content to sit reading in a library constructed in the tower from four in the morning until noon. Often he would retire for more hours of silent study at night, after the concert or play which invariably followed the main meal of the day. He studied ancient history and philosophy, read Latin and Greek authors in French translation, acquired a genuine interest in science and was soon able to pride himself on a comprehensive knowledge of French literature and speculative thought. Within forty-eight hours of moving into Rheinsberg Frederick had written an essay on the post-Cartesian speculations of Christian Wolff which he sent, with a fittingly diffident and flattering letter, to Voltaire at Cirey, on the borders of Lorraine. For the past decade Voltaire had been accepted by the intellectuals of western Europe as the greatest thinker of the age. It was therefore gratifying for Frederick to receive a reply, post-haste from Cirey, in which Voltaire complimented him on his learning and praised him as 'a most marvellous rarity' among princes. A correspondence began which was to continue for forty-two years, despite quarrels and political differences.

There is no doubt that Frederick absorbed a remarkable amount of reading material and yet he still found time to compose verse, enjoy music and write earnest essays. He was not, however, inclined to persevere with matters which seemed to him of little value, and he soon became as prejudiced as his mentor, Voltaire. Since Frederick held the language of his father's subjects to be essentially barbaric and incapable of producing literature of merit, he continued to speak and write German 'like a coachman', as he confessed with ill-disguised complacency. He found himself similarly defeated by the grammatical illogicalities of the English language and was disappointed at being unable to read Locke and Newton in their original tongue. Yet when eventually he read the plays of Shakespeare in translation he felt no such regret at his inability to master English: he found them lacking in dramatic unity and classical form and declared roundly that they were fit only for export to the redskins of America. Although he had a sense of comedy, he despised all forms of literary romanticism as unworthy frivolity. As a young man of sixteen visiting Dresden, he had signed a letter home to his sister 'Frederick the Philosopher', and it was as a Philosopher Prince that he continued to see himself during his years at Rheinsberg.

Frederick's metaphysical speculations won unalloyed compliments from Voltaire, but they are of less interest today than his narrowly political writing. Despite Frederick William's remarkable resilience, it had become clear to his ministers that the King's health remained poor and they began to ensure their own future by making amends for past insults to the Crown Prince. Throughout his period of residence at Rheinsberg, Frederick therefore received regular letters from his old enemy Grumbkow, who until his death in 1739 kept him in touch with Prussia's external policy, sometimes sending him despatches from foreign envoys and copies of important instructions sent from Berlin. It was accordingly

A boating party at Rheinsberg painted by Knobelsdorff.

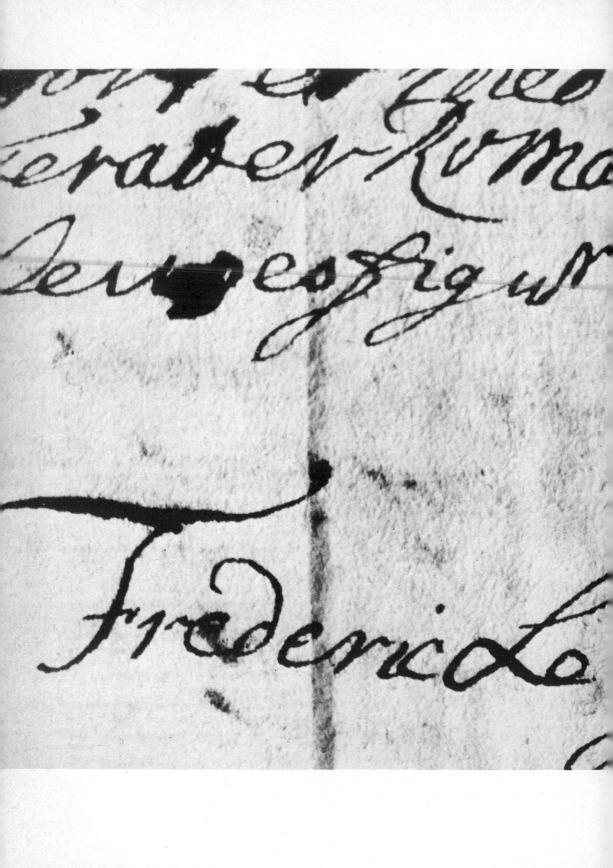

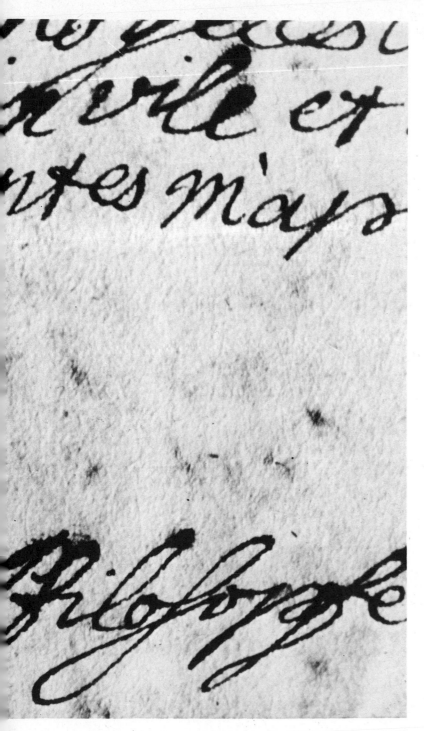

Frederick's letter to his sister Wilhelmina, signed 'Frederic le Philosophe'.

while cultivating tranquillity at Rheinsberg that Frederick began the practice of annotating official documents and of working out a consistent and ambitious foreign policy with which he would stagger his contemporaries as soon as he succeeded to the throne.

The diplomatic landscape, as viewed from Rheinsberg, looked deceptively familiar. For the past two centuries Germany and much of central Europe had been dominated by the House of Habsburg, ruling directly over Austria and indirectly, through election as Holy Roman Emperors, over the German-speaking lands as a whole. But in 1720 the succession to the Habsburg titles was thrown in doubt: Charles VI's heir was his three-year-old daughter, Maria Theresa, and it was not clear how many of his territories could pass to a woman. She could certainly not be elected to the Imperial title, and Charles therefore devoted his principal efforts for the next twenty years to ensuring that she succeeded to the exclusively Habsburg lands – the Archduchy of Austria (together with Styria, Carinthia and the Tyrol), the Bohemian Crown lands (Moravia, Silesia and Bohemia proper), the Austrian Netherlands (Belgium), Lombardy (and certain other possessions in northern Italy) and the lands of the Hungarian Crown (which had never in the past accepted succession in the female line). To safeguard Maria Theresa's claims and prevent dismemberment of the Habsburg inheritance, Emperor Charles VI issued a document known as the 'Pragmatic Sanction', originally drafted even before his daughter's birth but not made public until April 1720. The Pragmatic Sanction asserted the indivisibility of Charles's dominions and proclaimed his eldest daughter as sole inheritrix. Within five years it was accepted by representative assemblies for all Charles's lands, although the Hungarian Diet insisted on a number of constitutional concessions, and throughout the 1720s and 1730s the prime objective of Austrian diplomacy was to secure international recognition of the Sanction. As a secondary objective, Charles VI sought the backing of the powers for the election of Francis of Lorraine as Holy Roman Emperor: he had been brought up in Vienna and was a childhood sweetheart of Maria Theresa, whom he married in 1738. All the major European states except Bavaria eventually accorded recognition of the Pragmatic Sanction, but few were prepared to commit themselves to supporting Francis at the next Imperial election. The unresolved problems of the Habsburg succession were to give Frederick the opportunity for making a dramatic entry on the European stage as soon as he had come to the throne.

King Frederick William had pledged his support for the Pragmatic Sanction as early as 1725. He hoped that, in return for his favours, Charles VI would secure the cession to Brandenburg–Prussia of the duchies of Jülich and Berg, so as to strengthen the Hohenzollern position on the lower Rhine. But Charles, knowing that Frederick William was by conviction a dutiful upholder·of the Imperial system, did nothing about Jülich-Berg or any other territories which might have benefited Prussia strategically or commercially. Frederick William was angry. He was heard to complain that the Emperor treated him like a dog and he considered an approach to Austria's enemy, France, but the French showed him no more respect than the Austrians and when the Emperor recalled him to his old allegiance, predictably – like a dog – he obeyed. But things were changing, even at Potsdam, for to the surprise of his courtiers, Frederick William suddenly pointed to his son and exclaimed, with fervent parental pride, 'There goes one who will avenge me.'

Frederick was certainly not inclined to walk dutifully to heel. He had no intention of holding in check his natural independence of spirit for the sake of an Emperor, a Sanction or that amiable young man, Francis of Lorraine, whom he had met at his betrothal ceremonies. From his experiences in the Rhineland campaign and from what he read in the documents Grumbkow sent him, Frederick had come to think little of the Empire as an institution or of the Habsburgs as a German necessity. The European scene did not look the same from the library tower at Rheinsberg as from the palace at Potsdam. He saw current problems set against a historical background and in the last three years of his father's reign he wrote two books in which he sought to reconcile the philosophic analyses of the Enlightenment with his own consciousness of practical politics. Both works are as much dialogues with himself as serious contributions to knowledge, although he was not aware that in putting pen to paper he was primarily trying to clarify his own thoughts and doubts of conscience.

The earliest of these historical essays, *Consideration on the Present Political Condition of Europe*, was written in the winter of 1737-8 and reflected his concern with the Austro–French lack of interest in Jülich and Berg. It is an ambitious undertaking: an attempt to predict the future by tracing an unbroken chain of cause and effect in the behaviour of the European courts over several centuries. 'The policies of the great monarchies are virtually changeless in character. Their basic principle has always been to grasp every-

OPPOSITE The title page of
Frederick's philosophical
treatise *Antimachiavel*.

thing in order to expand territorially', he wrote, 'Their wisdom
consists in forestalling their enemies by playing a subtler game.'
The two richest and most powerful nations, France and England,
would continue to rival each other, although the contest would be
determined at sea rather than on land since the English were only
interested in continental ventures when they had a Marlborough
to lead them. The Dutch, he thought, were nowadays solely concerned with farming and commerce, while the Russian Empire was
an inchoate mass only partially organized into a state and impeding
the natural mechanism of historical causation by mere chance.
Austria, he maintained, was asserting an Imperial splendour which
she had not the means to maintain and was ignoring her true
European mission, which was to keep the Turkish hordes away
from the heart of the continent. Austria's weakness would be
shown when the Emperor Charles VI died: that would be the
moment for Europe's courts to undertake important ventures. But,
as though to hide his personal ambitions, Frederick decided to
end his essay on a high moral note: let rulers abandon the
selfish power politics into which their passions have led them,
and let them seek only the true princely duty of maintaining
the happiness of their subjects. 'To lose parts of one's kingdom',
he concludes, 'is a shameful humiliation, but to seek to conquer
lands to which one has no legal right is an act of injustice and
criminal robbery.'

This tone of moral indignation ran through Frederick's second
work, which was originally called *A Refutation of Machiavelli's
'Prince'*, but was renamed, at Voltaire's suggestion, *Antimachiavel*.
Basically Frederick was concerned to show that the petty states
and primitive monarchies depicted by Machiavelli in the early
sixteenth century were institutions of the past, and that the
doctrines of self-interest which Machiavelli had upheld as sound
advice for a prince were no longer applicable to the enlightened
ideals of the eighteenth century. A monarch today, Frederick
argued, was supported by a standing army and an organized
administration: he had no need to fear a rebellion of the nobility,
while a new view of life was freeing the State from the danger of
impassioned religious conflict. Hence the good Prince in the second
quarter of the eighteenth century must seek, not new conquests,
but the well-being of his people and the promotion of the arts and
pure science. The main argument was in many ways a continuation
of the *Reflections*. Yet there is a greater sophistication in *Antimachiavel* than in Frederick's earlier work. 'It is a political error

62

EXAMEN
DU PRINCE
DE
MACHIAVEL,
AVEC DES NOTES
Historiques & Politiques.

D. Coster inv.   J Basret fecit

A LA HAYE,
Chez JEAN VAN DUREN,
M. D. CC. XLI.
Avec Privilége.

to practise deceit', he wrote – but he added as an afterthought, 'if deceit is carried too far.'

While Frederick was writing the *Antimachiavel* it became clear he would soon himself be a reigning prince. Frederick William's health declined rapidly in the early months of 1740: this time he had not the strength to rally. Having inspected his coffin and given detailed instructions for his funeral, he at last 'had the decency to die' on 31 May 1740. An hour later his old counsellors dutifully knelt at Frederick's feet. The doyen among them, Prince Leopold of Anhalt-Dessau, who had been in effect War Minister for more than a quarter of a century, assured the new King of his personal devotion, hoping that His Majesty would graciously permit him to retain his posts and authority. Fredcrick, helping the old man to his feet, duly confirmed him in office: 'But as for authority', he added, 'I do not know what you mean. In this kingdom, I am the only person to exercise authority.' A new reign had indeed begun.

OPPOSITE A sentimental view of Frederick kneeling to receive his dying father's blessing.

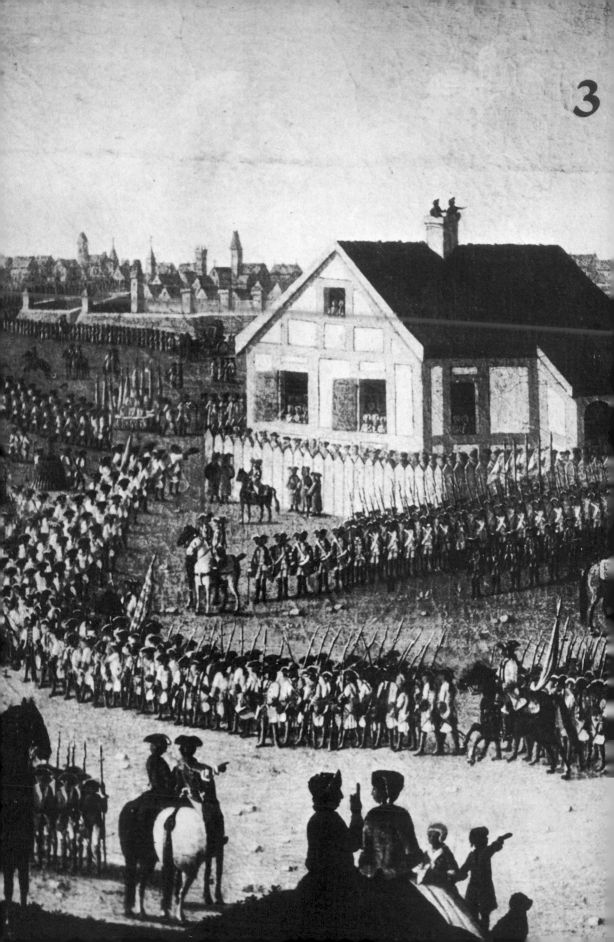

Rendezvous with Glory

FOREIGN ENVOYS AT BERLIN assumed that Frederick's accession meant a complete break with the recent past. So, for that matter, did anyone else who knew the King well. For the past four years visitors to Rheinsberg had noted that the principal decorative motif of the château held out promise in every room of a golden future: thus in one fresco Aurora magnificently dispersed the clouds while, next door, Phoebus stood proudly rampant in his chariot. Now, in these first June days of 1740, Frederick's friends and intimates confidently waited for classical allegory to step down from the walls and bathe Prussia in the radiance of a new day. To them it was unthinkable that this 'Solomon of the North' (as Voltaire proleptically hailed Frederick) would be content with the old order and tired men of his father's twenty-seven years on the throne. Never before had a change of ruler in Brandenburg Prussia aroused so eager an air of expectancy.

The opening weeks of the reign seemed almost to justify these extravagant hopes. Frederick proclaimed the abolition of torture for civilian offenders, the freeing of books and periodicals from censorship, the right of all religious professions to practise their beliefs, and the disbandment of Frederick William's personal body-guard of giant grenadiers, the old King's one expensive luxury. At the same time Frederick ordered the opening of royal granaries to relieve a scarcity of bread and he began to draw up plans for de-foresting some of the Crown hunting reserves, believing the land could be better used for profitable purposes. All these measures made good sense and confirmed the King's popularity with the mass of his subjects. He declared he had no wish for an elaborate coronation – 'A crown', he remarked, 'is merely a hat that lets the rain in' – but he insisted on travelling to Königsberg and to Cleves in order to receive formal homage from the provincial deputies. A similar ceremony was carried out in Berlin. On this occasion Frederick, departing from tradition, came out on the palace balcony and stood there for half an hour, hardly moving and saying not a word, as the crowd below cheered their new sovereign. No doubt their enthusiasm was heightened by a liberal distribution of gold and silver medallions, but it was a significant innovation.

His Rheinsberg friends were less pleased. They had hoped their past loyalty would be rewarded; the best of them also looked forward to the coming of a golden age for music and all the arts and sciences. Frederick did indeed find posts at Court for those who had stood by him in the difficult years, but none of these

PREVIOUS PAGES The surrender of Breslau to Frederick in 1742.

68

EDICT.

Wegen

der wieder hergestelleten

CENSUR,

derer

in Königl. Landen heraus kommenden

Bücher und Schrifften,

wie auch

wegen des Debits ärgerlicher Bücher,
so ausserhalb Landes verleget werden.

De Dato, Berlin den 11ten May, 1749.

BERLIN,
Gedruckt bey dem Königlichen Preußischen Hof-Buchdrucker,
Christian Albrecht Gäbert.

Although Frederick's reign began with a great display of liberalism, he became increasingly conservative. This edict, issued in 1749, re-imposed the harsh censorship which he had relaxed when he first became King.

appointments carried with them either power or political responsibility. The King invited Knobelsdorff to prepare plans for an opera house in Berlin, and he reconstituted the Prussian Academy of Science, sending invitations to distinguished foreign scholars whom his father had ignored or humiliated. He did not, however, spend money liberally as a patron of culture. His father's frugality had ensured for him a happily full treasury at his accession, but he had his own ideas on the use he should make of his resources.

Punishments in eighteenth-
century Prussia were brutal
and appalling. One of the
first acts of Frederick's
reign was to abolish the use
of torture for civilian
offenders. LEFT A hard
labour prison. BELOW A
formal military flogging and
RIGHT wives being beaten
for unfaithfulness.

Neither his father's ex-ministers nor his own intimates could read his intentions.

Eleven weeks after his accession Frederick set out on a leisurely journey to his sister Wilhelmina, at Bayreuth, and his Rhenish outposts around Cleves. It was intended, in the first instance, as a tour of pleasure rather than of business. Frederick told Voltaire he hoped to cross into the Austrian Netherlands and meet him in Brussels. He also arranged a surprise visit, incognito, to the city of Strasbourg, the only occasion in his life on which he set foot on French soil. Although the city governor was mildly embarrassed by the popular reception given to this thinly disguised foreign traveller, the escapade was harmless enough. It confirmed the widespread impression that Frederick was a light-hearted adventurer, uninhibited by formal protocol.

What followed was far more ominous. For eight years Prussian troops had occupied the small town and castle at Herstal, a strategic position on the left bank of the Maas in what is nowadays Belgium. The inhabitants of Herstal regarded themselves as vassals of the Prince-Bishop of Liège and refused to take an oath of fealty to the new Prussian King. They had the support not only of the Prince-Bishop, but of the Emperor Charles VI and Louis XV of France as well. Frederick had no wish to retain an isolated garrison on the Maas, but he was determined to use the Herstal Question as a means of impressing his neighbours by a show of strength. While he was at Wesel, on his Westphalian journey, he gave orders for a punitive expedition to be mounted against the Prince-Bishop: three battalions of Guards and a squadron of Dragoons were to seize Maaseik, one of the episcopal towns; they would publish a manifesto drawn up by Frederick denouncing the Herstal 'rebels' and await a response from Liège. The whole affair looks, in retrospect, anachronistically modern.

The Maaseik expedition set out on 11 September and by the evening of 14 September its task was accomplished. The Prince-Bishop protested, so did Charles VI. Frederick ignored their shocked susceptibilities. He told the Bishop he would withdraw his troops from Maaseik and give up his claim to Herstal in return for payment of 240,000 thalers. After six weeks of negotiation the money was duly handed over and the Prussian soldiery left both towns. It was an arrogant display of sword-rattling, intended to demonstrate that the new ruler in Brandenburg–Prussia was not going to be 'treated like a dog'. On Frederick's personal instructions, his envoy to Paris informed Louis XV, in an apparent confidence, that his master was quite likely to 'put all Europe to the torch' for the sake of his legitimate rights. 'All Europe' reserved its judgement, but noted that along with his enlightened reforms at home, Frederick had also authorized his ministers to raise seventeen new battalions of infantry, two fresh squadrons of cavalry and a regiment of hussars.

The Herstal Question ruled out any visit to Brussels. But Frederick was able to meet Voltaire, as he had hoped. For three days the two men exchanged flattering compliments at Schloss Moyland, near Cleves, the brilliance of their table-talk marred for the King by a sudden attack of fever. 'We supped together, discussing at some length the immortality of the soul, freedom, and Plato's hermaphrodites', wrote Voltaire afterwards. 'He has', declared Frederick in a private letter, 'the eloquence of Cicero, the gentleness of Pliny, the wisdom of Agrippa.' Yet, despite the profusion of hyperbole, there was on both sides a certain reserve. The three days which the temperamentally anti-militarist Voltaire spent at Schloss Moyland coincided exactly in time with the Maaseik expedition. A week later Voltaire wrote, 'Almost he made me forget that I saw, sitting at the foot of my bed, a sovereign who had under his command an army of a hundred thousand men.' Given the place and the date of this first encounter, a wealth of significance lies in that word 'almost'. It was far easier for the philosophizing King and the kingly philosopher to share great thoughts by letter than around the table of a fortified castle.

Cardinal Fleury, the veteran foreign minister of Louis xv, suspected that Frederick's exaggerated concern with Herstal and Maaseik showed that he would soon re-open the Jülich-Berg Question. For the moment, however, it seemed doubtful if he would survive long enough to raise any diplomatic question whatsoever. He found it impossible to shake off his fever so long as he was on the Rhine and even when he returned to Brandenburg he continued to suffer from fits of ague. Wilhelmina, who had come on a visit from Bayreuth, and his close friend Fredersdorf were alarmed. In the fourth week of October they persuaded him to travel to Rheinsberg, hoping he might recuperate there. Five days later surprising news reached him. On 26 October Frederick himself described what had happened in a letter to Voltaire:

A most unforeseen event prevents me from chattering to you as I would wish. The Emperor is dead. His demise has put an end to all my peaceful ideas. I think it will now be a matter of gunpowder, soldiers and trenches rather than of actresses, ballets and the theatre . . . The

The great philosopher
Voltaire who was a life-long,
though quarrelsome friend
of Frederick, and his guest
at Potsdam.

moment has come for a complete change in the old political system . . . I
am casting aside my fever, for in these circumstances I need command of
my whole self.

The King rightly assumed that Charles VI's sudden death would
throw Germany and central Europe into confusion. There was so
much unrest in the traditional Habsburg lands that it was unlikely
that Maria Theresa's succession would go unchallenged, despite

74

the lip-service already paid by Europe's sovereigns to the Pragmatic Sanction. Moreover, even if Maria Theresa were acknowledged as Archduchess of Austria and Queen of Hungary, who would be the new Emperor? Frederick summoned to Rheinsberg his chief specialist on foreign affairs, Count von Podewils, and his most trusted regimental commander, General von Schwerin. Together the three men began to examine ways of exploiting the situation to Prussia's advantage. Frederick was no longer interested in comparatively unimportant territories on the lower Rhine: the rich province of Silesia was the prize he coveted. Before he had reached a final decision on policy, a courier arrived from St Petersburg with the equally staggering news that the Empress Anna had suffered a fatal stroke. Thus, within ten days, the Habsburg titles passed to a woman of twenty-four (three months pregnant), while an infant four months old became nominal Autocrat of All the Russias. Less than half a year after his own accession, Frederick found himself master of the only stable power in Europe east of the Rhine, with a well-equipped and numerically strong army ready to impose his will. Silesia seemed to Frederick a ripe plum which would fall into his hands at the first shaking of the tree.

Podewils, the son-in-law and successor of the cautious Grumbkow, urged restraint: offer military and diplomatic assistance to Maria Theresa in return for a promise of the future cession of Silesia, he urged. But Frederick calculated that, if he was to secure the province, he must march first and negotiate later: his army would strike in the south while the Russians were incapable of helping Maria Theresa by action on his eastern frontier. Strategically this was sound reasoning: the Hohenzollerns had a tenuous claim to some small areas in Silesia (though the Great Elector had renounced the last of these feudal rights in 1686) and Podewils was busy making out of them a plausible case for foreign consumption; but Frederick knew that the diplomats in Vienna would take little notice of any formal statement of demands. He began to concentrate an army near the Silesian border in the first days of December. Only after the regiments were at their war-stations did he send an offer to Maria Theresa, pledging her his support and his vote for her husband as Emperor, provided that Silesia was handed over to Brandenburg–Prussia in its entirety. Before any reply could reach him from Vienna, he had given his generals their marching orders. 'Gentlemen', he told them on 12 December, 'I have no allies save your valour and your goodwill . . . Our cause is just . . . Farewell until we achieve the rendezvous with

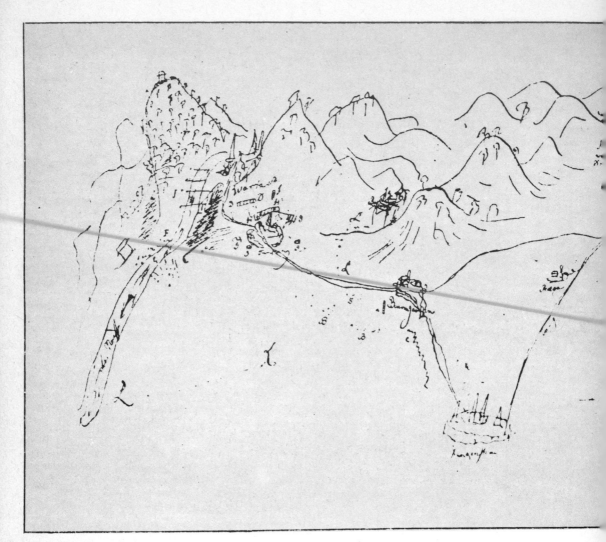

glory which awaits us.' On 16 December Frederick led his troops in person across the frontier, an army of forty thousand men, more than ten times the size of the defending garrisons. A solemn proclamation, posted in every town which his army entered, told the people of Silesia that the King of Prussia was marching southwards to protect Maria Theresa's dominions from her numerous enemies. Within six weeks the whole of Silesia, except for three isolated fortresses, was in Frederick's possession.

Maria Theresa had no intention of bargaining with Frederick: 'We shall have no words to exchange with your master so long as a single Prussian soldier remains on the soil of Silesia', she induced her consort Francis, to say on her behalf to Frederick's envoy,

ABOVE One of Frederick's own sketches of his plan to invade Silesia.

ABOVE RIGHT Podewils, Frederick's First Minister: a man who gave his loyalty to Frederick, but who frequently found himself powerless because of Frederick's passion for running the country himself.

excusing herself from personally receiving him because of her advanced pregnancy. It was, however, easier to strike noble attitudes in Vienna than to raise an army and find a competent commander. Hence it was not until the end of March 1741 that Marshal Neipperg (whom Charles VI had imprisoned for surrendering Belgrade to the Turks) was given a chance to redeem his reputation by crossing into Lower Silesia from Bohemia and threatening the main Prussia positions around the city of Breslau (Wroclaw). The weather was atrocious, a blizzard sweeping down on the wooded hills as late as 9 April. The following day the two armies met at Mollwitz, twenty-four miles south-east of Breslau. It was Frederick's first battle, and a crucial one: unless his troops could break the

77

Austrian enveloping movement, he would be cut off from Berlin.

Mollwitz was not the 'rendezvous with glory' which their hot-headed young sovereign had promised the Prussian generals on the eve of the campaign. Faced with the imminent reality of an engagement with an experienced commander, Frederick lost some of his ardour. He spent two sleepless nights waiting for the snow to ease sufficiently for the cavalry to move forward. At times he suffered premonitions of death and he sent farewell messages to his heir (his brother Augustus William), to his sister and his Rheinsberg friends. Characteristically he made no mention of his wife. When eventually the weather cleared he led his troops forward carefully and methodically, as all the textbooks recommended. It was too good an opportunity for Neipperg to miss. A cavalry charge threw the Prussians into confusion and there was a real danger that Frederick himself would be killed. Schwerin, who had watched Frederick's preparations with ill-concealed impatience, urged him to escape and rally the Prussian reserves. Frederick rode more than fifty miles that day, narrowly escaping capture by the Austrians. When next morning an outrider from Schwerin caught up with the King, he brought the bitterly gratifying news that, in Frederick's absence, his generals had gained a remarkable victory. The Prussian infantry, carefully drilled for twenty years by Frederick William's instructors, had easily dispersed the hastily improvised Austrian army.

The rival armies continued to face each other throughout the summer of 1741, neither commander prepared to risk a second encounter after such a closely fought battle. Yet, though Mollwitz was far from being a spectacular feat of arms for Frederick personally, it won him the political reputation he sought in the European capitals. All the contenders for the Habsburg lands – the French, the Bavarians, the Savoyards, the Saxons, even the King of Spain and the Pope – had to re-shape their policy so as to fit Prussia into their calculations. Within eight weeks of Mollwitz, the French had concluded an alliance with Prussia and were preparing an invasion of Austria in support of Charles Albert of Bavaria's claims to the Imperial title. While stalemate reigned in Silesia, Maria Theresa's enemies besieged Prague, captured Linz and threatened Vienna itself: she summoned the Hungarian Diet and appealed to it, as Hungary's crowned Queen, to save the throne and the dynasty. Mollwitz had turned a Silesian campaign into the War of the Austrian Succession.

The French had no wish to see their Prussian ally become all-powerful in Germany, for it was no advantage to Versailles to humble the Habsburgs and elevate the Hohenzollerns: balanced discontent between the Germanic dynasties was a key principle of French policy. Frederick, for his part, did not want to encourage Louis xv to increase his influence east of the Rhine and the upper Danube; and he had no intention of losing his freedom of diplomatic initiative as part of a French-dominated coalition. In October 1741 he accordingly held secret talks with Neipperg in the isolated castle of Kleinschnellendorf, in the hills south of Mollwitz. There the opposing commanders agreed on a secret armistice: the Prussians would go through the motions of laying siege to the picturesque town of Neisse for a fortnight, while Neipperg withdrew his main forces to prepare for a counter-offensive along the Danube against the French and Bavarian invaders. Neisse would then be surrendered to the Prussians, who would be left in control of all Silesia. By such a dubious means, undertaken without reference to his ministers or field commanders, Frederick believed he would restore a balance in central Europe while retaining the prime

The appalling conditions of eastern Europe in winter have been the ruin of more than one general: Prussian troops in a Silesian town.

79

MARIÆ THERESIÆ RE GINÆ SVÆ CLEMENTISSIMÆ

HUNGARIA
DEVOTISSIMA

Armata est quando pro me tua Dextera ferro
HUngare, sors poterum hoc nulla Sinistra rapit.

objective of his own campaign. The author of the *Antimachiavel* had out-Machiavelled his contemporaries in statecraft. Yet it is an open question whether, in the long run, his cleverness proved an asset. Since the Neisse bargain could hardly be kept secret, his credibility as an ally was destroyed. After Kleinschnellendorf neither Maria Theresa nor the French and Bavarians trusted him – and with good reason.

OPPOSITE The Empress, Maria Theresa, Queen of Hungary, who was to have many quarrels with Frederick.

If Frederick hoped to step aside from the war which his greed had precipitated, he was disappointed, for the campaigns that winter failed to follow any predictable pattern. Less than three weeks after the Kleinschnellendorf agreement, Prague fell to a Franco–Bavarian force and all Bohemia passed into the hands of Charles Albert of Bavaria. Hurriedly Frederick re-adjusted his policy: he did not want to see a powerful Franco–Bavarian army on the borders of Silesia, and he therefore agreed to support Charles Albert's election as Emperor in return for the cession of a segment of Bohemia around Glatz (nowadays the Polish town of Klodzko) and a free hand to invade Moravia, despite the secret armistice he had made with Neipperg two months earlier. The key Moravian fortress of Olmütz fell to the Prussians before the end of the year and, with Frederick's cavalry patrols sweeping southwards down the valleys, there seemed momentarily a possibility that Vienna would be invaded. But Maria Theresa was not unduly alarmed: winter was on her side, and a powerful Austrian and Hungarian army began to carry the war back into Germany proper. On 24 February 1742, Charles Albert of Bavaria was crowned Emperor of Frankfurt, styling himself Charles VII, the first non-Habsburg to wear the Imperial Crown for over three hundred years; but, as though to mock his pretensions, on that same day Maria Theresa's troops entered Munich, the Bavarian capital. Small wonder if Frederick, poised uncertainly in Moravia, suspected he was backing the wrong side. His sister Wilhelmina had gone to Frankfurt for the coronation, and her letters to Frederick let him see how low was her opinion of Charles VII's abilities and prospects. Once again all Prussian military operations were halted while desultory peace talks began between Frederick's envoys and the Austrian commanders. This time, however, Maria Theresa was in no hurry to conclude an armistice: another battle might avenge Mollwitz and suitably repay Frederick for his treachery.

The military initiative was seized by her brother-in-law, Charles of Lorraine. In the spring of 1742 he took command of a well-equipped force, slightly superior in numbers to the Prussian

81

invaders, and set out to bring Frederick to battle. The rival armies met at Chotusitz, a village fifty miles south-east of Prague, on 17 May. It was a grimly bloody contest, with the Prussians withstanding four hours of cavalry assault before Frederick succeeded in enticing the Austrian horsemen into marshy ground south of the River Elbe where they were trapped and exposed to a series of counter-attacks from his infantry. Early in the afternoon Charles of Lorraine ordered his men to fall back: the Prussians pursued them for a few miles but were then halted at their King's insistence. Frederick had wanted to destroy the threat to his own army – and this was already achieved in front of Chotusitz itself – but he did not want to inflict so serious a defeat on the Austrians that the French alone were left with a powerful army in central Europe. It was enough for him that Chotusitz had inclined Maria Theresa to look favourably on his terms of peace.

By the Peace of Breslau of June 1742 (confirmed in a definitive treaty at Berlin a month later) Frederick withdrew from the war with almost all the territorial gains he had sought. His envoys asked for Silesia and recognition of the annexation of the Glatz region, and, to their surprise, the Austrians met most of these demands though there was haggling over the precise line of the frontier. English mediation had apparently ensured that the 'Queen of Hungary', as Frederick always called Maria Theresa, was more generously disposed towards Prussia than he had anticipated. She said nothing of a settlement with his allies and, once again, he was not especially concerned with their susceptibilities. In reality, as Frederick was shrewd enough to suspect, she had resolved to settle the major conflict with France and Bavaria before turning in vengeance against the despoiler of Silesia. In her eyes, there was nothing final about the Treaty of Berlin: it discredited Frederick with her other enemies and it removed from the field of battle the well-disciplined and well-trained Prussian army. She would deal with Prussia in isolation, at a time of Austria's own choosing.

Frederick had few illusions about the Queen. An extended truce suited him admirably. Outwardly he seemed once again a man of peace: he returned to Berlin, took the waters to relieve the rheumatism he had contracted in his winter campaigns, and attended the opening ceremonies of the opera house which Knobelsdorff had completed while the King was at the wars. For two years Frederick was content to watch the Franco-Austrian struggle from the sidelines. His treasury benefited from the respite, and so did his army: by the summer of 1744 he had 120,000 men under arms, most of whom he had himself helped to put through rigorous battle training. No one believed the peace would be of long duration.

Often in the two-year interlude there was intensive diplomatic activity at Berlin and Potsdam. George II of England, marshalling a 'Pragmatic army' of British, Hanoverian, Dutch and Hessian troops in the closing months of 1742, hoped he might induce Frederick to join a coalition aimed at checking French influence east of the Rhine. But Frederick was more alarmed by the improvement in Maria Theresa's fortunes than by the activity of the French. He received the British diplomats courteously, but promised nothing. Louis xv, too, sought Prussian aid: he may even have subsidized a visit by Voltaire to Berlin in the hope that the man of letters might succeed in re-kindling Frederick's love for the French art of living. If this was, indeed, the purpose behind Voltaire's first journey to Berlin, it was unnecessary. The King of Prussia remained culturally an unrepentant Francophile, but this did not incline him to approve of the policies of Versailles. He did not wish to be the partner of either France or England: he would intervene in the war only as a champion of the German rulers and a defender of the Empire, against Habsburg or Bourbon ambitions.

By the summer of 1743 Maria Theresa's troops had ejected the French from Prague and advanced to the Rhine, threatening metropolitan France itself. Frederick became uneasy when he discovered that the treaties which she was concluding with Britain and Savoy contained a guarantee of Austria's frontiers as they had been in her father's reign, with Silesia a Habsburg possession. By the following summer he was so alarmed by Austria's continued run of successes that he resolved to re-enter the war, striking suddenly and unexpectedly in Bohemia. The Prussians announced that they were placing eighty thousand auxiliary troops at the disposal of Charles VII in order 'to restore liberty to the Empire, dignity to the Emperor and tranquillity to Europe'. With these unconvincing war aims Frederick crossed the frontier into Bohemia in August 1744 while the main Austrian forces were on the Rhine. Not a shot was fired against him until he reached Prague and even then he was able to take the Bohemian capital after only the briefest of sieges. At the end of September Frederick wrote exultantly to Podewils, 'Without actually flying through the clouds like Mercury with my troops, I have pressed forward my operations to the very frontier of Austria'.

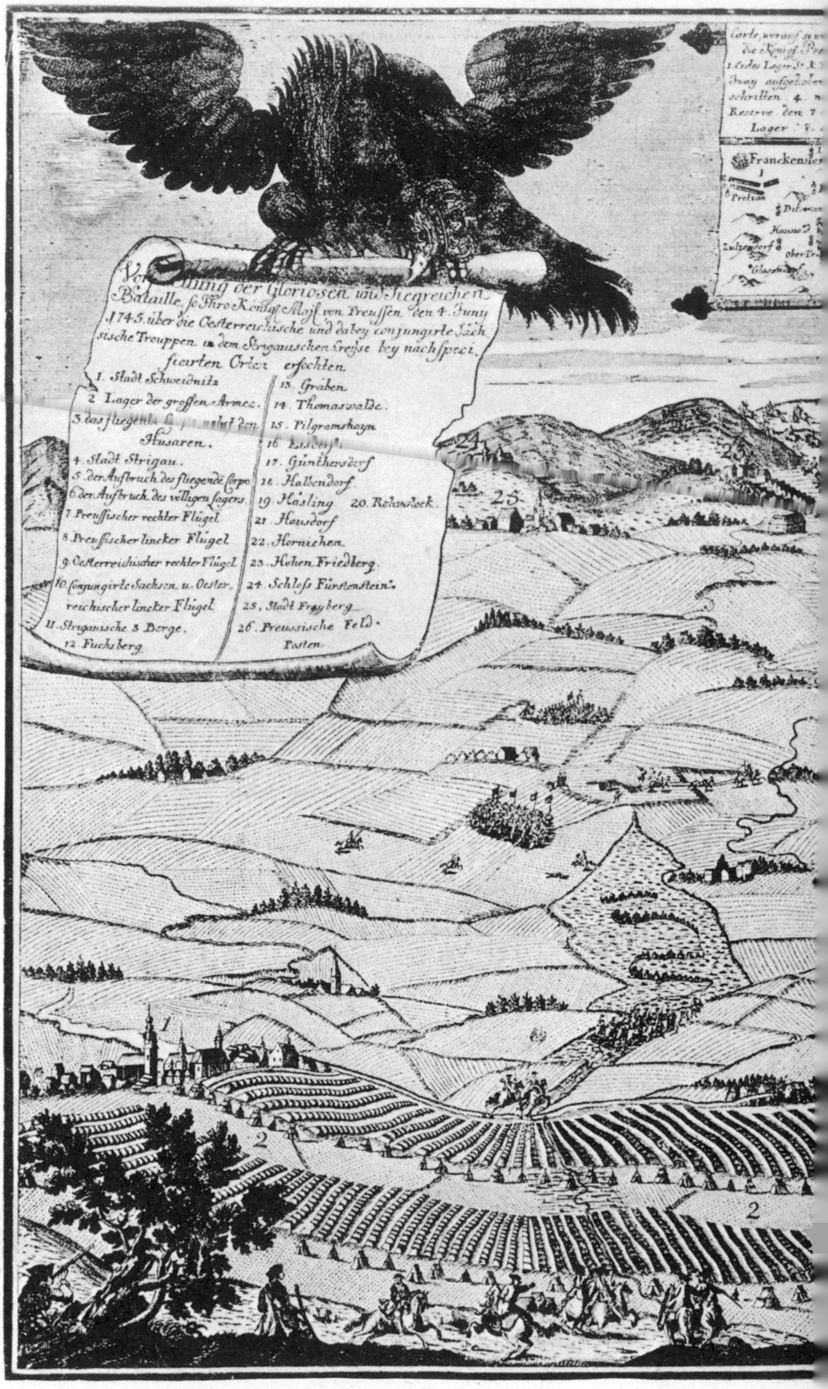
Bataille, so Ihro Königl. Majt. von Preussen den 4. Juny
1745. über die Oesterreichische und dabey conjungirte Säch
sische Trouppen in dem Strigauischen Creyse bey nachspeci
ficirten Orten erfochten
1. Stadt Schweidnitz
2. Lager der grossen Armee.
3. das fliegende ... Husaren.
4. Stadt Strigau.
5. der Aufbruch des fliegende Corpo
6. der Aufbruch des völligen Lagers.
7. Preussischer rechter Flügel
8. Preussischer lincker Flügel
9. Oesterreichischer rechter Flügel
10. conjungirte Sachsen u. Oesterreichischer lincker Flügel
11. Strigauische 3 Berge.
12. Fuchsberg
13. Graben
14. Thomaswalde.
15. Pilgramshayn
17. Güntersdorf
18. Halbendorf
19. Häsling
20. Rohnstock
21. Housdorf
22. Hornichen
23. Hohen Friedberg.
24. Schloss Fürstenstein.
25. Stadt Freyberg
26. Preussische Feld Posten
Franckenstein

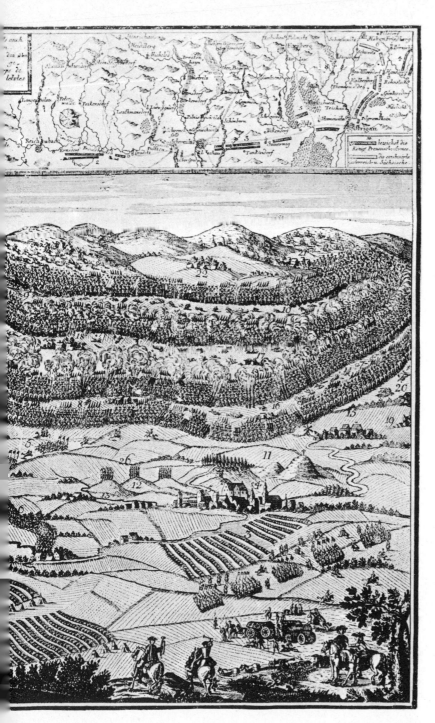

A plan of the battle of Hohenfriedberg, Frederick's 'mousetrap' and an overwhelming victory, which vindicated completely his unorthodox approach to fighting. The Prussian army is in the middle ground, and it is on the left of the picture that Frederick's cavalry broke through.

85

But Frederick was courting disaster. The French virtually disengaged their army along the Rhine, partly because severe illness curtailed Louis xv's political activity but also because it suited them to see the Austrians withdraw forces from western Germany in order to meet the challenge in Bohemia. A formidable army was thus able to appear suddenly that autumn on Frederick's western flank. The Austrian commanders refused to give him battle, preferring to move parallel along his line of march, waiting until the rain and the mud and the desolate countryside sapped Prussian morale. Hungarian horsemen raided Frederick's extended line of communications while the local peasantry remained sullen and unco-operative, some even forming what would later have been called 'partisan bands' in the forests. By the third week in October Frederick had realised the danger and began to shorten his lines, seeking to bring his men back north of the Elbe, which was itself in danger of flooding from the heavy rain. As winter set in, conditions became grimmer still. At the end of November a disconsolate army toiled northwards from Prague, heading for the mountain passes and the uncertain hospitality of Silesia. Seventeen thousand Prussians failed to keep up with the retreating army and were therefore accounted as deserters. By the end of the first week in December, Bohemia had been cleared of the Prussians and only the threat of snow and blizzard saved Prussian Silesia from immediate invasion. Frederick had sustained a major strategic defeat without once fighting a battle. Over-confidence and a total disregard of logistical problems exposed him to the risks which, on a larger scale, were to overwhelm Napoleon in 1812. An intensely proud army disintegrated into a rabble within a mere six weeks.

Fortunately for Frederick the fortresses of Silesia had been strengthened during the interlude of peace, and he had considerable reserves of trained men. He did not minimize his difficulties. He knew that Maria Theresa's army was commanded by Marshal Otto von Traun, a wily old fox perfectly capable of planning a march through Silesia and into Brandenburg with the coming of spring. Moreover it seemed likely that Saxony would support Maria Theresa and threaten Brandenburg from the south. Secretly Frederick gave orders to make ready the defences of Spandau, the principal fortress in the Berlin area. He was taking no chances now.

Oddly enough, a political misfortune freed him from military embarrassment. In January 1745 Emperor Charles died: his son was willing to give up all claims to the Empire and come to terms with the Habsburgs. Frederick could thus no longer pretend to be defending the rights of the German Princes and upholding the imperial constitution: he was now fighting a war for Prussia's survival, nothing more and nothing less. Since the French that year were primarily interested in chasing the English across the Low Countries, Prussia awaited the expected challenge in the spring alone and dangerously exposed. But Maria Theresa was eager for her husband's election as Emperor. She wanted the coronation city of Frankfurt made secure by the most competent of her generals and she therefore sent Traun to Frankfurt while handing over his army in Bohemia to her brother-in-law, Charles of Lorraine, in whose soldierly abilities she retained an undiscerning faith. Frederick, returning to the Silesian war zone from Berlin, learned of Traun's replacement with relief, even though he heard at the same time of Saxony's entry into the war. Immediately, he began to bait a mouse-trap for Charles – the metaphor is Frederick's own.

At the end of May, Prince Charles was gratified to discover that the whole Prussian army was drawn up in the plains thirty miles west of Breslau around the village of Striegau and below the Sudeten foothills. On 3 June Charles established his headquarters at a neighbouring village, Hohenfriedburg, where he had a panoramic view of the Prussian position. Frederick, however, completely fooled him by a feint movement of troops to the north-east shortly before dusk. At dawn on the following morning the Prussians launched a surprise attack on the Saxon forward positions well to the west. Before Prince Charles was put on the alert the Prussian heavy cavalry had fallen on the principal Austrian defensive lines, the King personally leading a charge on the Austrian cannons. By nine in the morning the battle of Hohenfriedberg was over. Prince Charles lost seven thousand Austro-Saxon dead and another six thousand men taken prisoner (together with sixty-six cannon): the Prussians sustained less than a thousand fatal casualties.

Frederick was justly proud of his mouse-trap, maintaining at the time that Europe had seen no comparable victory since Blenheim. Certainly Hohenfriedberg had more of the ring of military 'glory' he had promised his generals than any of the previous episodes in the conquest of Silesia. But, though Hohenfriedberg safeguarded Silesia and ruled out any incursions into Brandenburg, it did not end the campaign. Prince Charles of Lorraine's army still held the principal positions in Bohemia, ready to fall on Frederick's troops if they penetrated too rashly into the mountain chain. For a

moment, on the last day of September, it seemed that Charles's opportunity had come: the Prussians, outnumbered nearly two to one by the Prince's army, were surprised by a dawn attack in the valley of Soor. Had Frederick fallen back, as all the military text-books taught, he would have been ambushed by a second Austrian force: he chose instead to go against the rules of warfare and order his cavalry to attack uphill. It was a far more murderous battle than Hohenfriedberg, but against the odds Frederick ended the day victorious, his reputation as a military commander redeemed. Yet still Maria Theresa would not make peace, so long as the army of Saxony was in the field. Only when old Leopold of Anhalt-Dessau, Frederick William's companion-in-arms, defeated the Saxons at Kesselsdorf outside Dresden on 15 December would the 'Queen of Hungary' authorize peace overtures to Frederick.

The war ended for Frederick, fittingly enough, on Christmas Day 1745. All he sought was a re-affirmation of the settlement made three years before at Breslau. By the Treaty of Dresden, Maria Theresa once again conceded that Silesia and Glatz were part of the kingdom of Prussia while Frederick formally recognized her husband, Francis, as Emperor. Both rivals were sick of war and all its tragedy 'From now on', declared Frederick when he returned to Berlin, 'I will not even throw anything at a cat except in self-defence . . . To put it briefly, I want simply to enjoy life.' At the time he meant what he said.

OPPOSITE Marshal von Traun, Maria Theresa's crafty old commander.

89

4
The Palace
Free from Care

FREDERICK ARRIVED BACK IN BERLIN from the peacemaking ceremonies at Dresden in the closing days of 1745 to find himself treated as an almost legendary figure. Only a few months before, there had been a serious danger of the enemy reaching the city, which was less than forty miles from the Saxon frontier. It seemed then as if the whole Silesian adventure would bring to the state nothing but agony and bankruptcy. But all that was now forgotten. His subjects, taking their cue from Voltaire, welcomed their King as 'Frederick the Great'. He had conquered and safe-guarded a valuable province with so many inhabitants that the total population of Brandenburg–Prussia was increased by almost half. Henceforth the kingdom of Prussia would be respected as a major European power, freed from vassalage to the Habsburgs and able to claim at least an equal voice with the archaic Empire in the affairs of the continent. Small wonder if the diminutive figure, with the shabby uniform and reddish unpolished boots, was accorded a hero's welcome by his loyal Berliners.

In appearance and character he was not the type of man whom romantics idolize. It did not worry him. Though he possessed a talent for publicity with his pen, he never thought highly of public approbation, nor did it occur to him to make any appeal to the multitude. As the carriage bore him through the streets of Berlin in the fading light of that December day, he sat huddled on an open seat facing his two brothers Augustus William and Henry, saying nothing to them and solemnly saluting the cheering crowds. When he reached the palace, he turned towards his well-wishers, re-moved his hat and stood silently facing them, with no more emotion showing in his expression than when he had unex-pectedly stepped out on the balcony soon after his accession. It appears, from what he later wrote and said, that he was well pleased with his reception, but his strange sense of royal dignity prevented him from sharing in any outward display of rejoicing by his subjects. 'Put a monkey on a camel and you'll get much the same response', he once remarked disdainfully after a similar show of public acclaim at Breslau.

This ready acceptance of monarchical solitude became a marked characteristic of Frederick's nature as he passed from youth to middle age. No doubt it was, in part, a consequence of the humilia-tions of his childhood and adolescence; he retained throughout life a self-protective bitterness which at times would shoot maliciously through all his human relationships. He enjoyed good talk in pleasant company but, increasingly as he grew older, his

PREVIOUS PAGES A view of Sans Souci during its construction.

92

Jhro Königl. Majestæ in Preussen, wie solche, im Somer in begleitung Sr. Hoheit des Prinzen Heinrichs, in dero Phaeton mit 8 Pferden, besuchen die 5 Parades in Berlin gehalten

A. Der König. B. Prinz Heinrich. C. Vor Leib Pagen in rothen Sammet mit Gold u. Drap d'Or Westen. D. Zwey Cavalier Husaren deren Mäntel u. Westen von Ponceau Samet, reich mit Gold galonirt die Camisöhler aber von roth u. goldenen Procat. E. 4 Laüffer so ebenfals in Ponceau Samet mit Gold bekleidet seyn F. Wacht Parade des ehemahligen Aufrüngschen jetz Widdel Infanterie Regiments. G. der Major welcher den König salutirt H. der Chef des Regiments den König ervartend. 1. die Kaufmanns Börse 2. die neue Packhoff 3. der Bran 4. des Kaufmanns und Cotton Fabricant Oehmichens Haus 5. das Feld Marschall Linger- sche Haus. 6. neue Häuser in der Sophien Stadt. 7. Sophien Kirche.

Sa Majesté Prusienne, frequentant en Eté, dans son nouveau Phaeton attelé de 8 Chevaux, les cinq Parades de Berlin avec Son Altesse le Prince Henry

A. le Roy. B. le Prince Henry. C. le 4 premiers Pages, habillés en Velour rouge à Westes et Pourpoints de Drap d'or. D. deux Ufficiers de Corpe Manteau et Culottes Velour rouge, richement galonné, le Camisole de Brocat rouge à Or. E. 4 Coureurs habillés en Velour rouge et en Pourpoint du Regiment de Widel G. le Major qui fait la Salutation au Roy avec son Epée. H. le Chef du Regiment attendant le Roy. 1. la Bourse des Marchands 2. la Douane 3. Ma- chine pour lever les Ballots hors des Navires 4. Maison du Negotiant et Fabricant des Cottons Oemike. 5. Maison de Feld-Marechall Linger. 6. Maisons nouveaux dans la Ville nommé de Sophie. 7. l'Eglise de Sophie

power of friendship was limited by consciousness of his own social and intellectual isolation. Constantly he felt forced to hold personal emotions in check, adopting towards even his closest associates a coldly sardonic tone, rather than permit any show of sentimentality or affection. By the time he returned from his Silesian Wars two of his Rheinsberg friends – Jordan and Keyserlingk – were dead and his old, well-loved tutor Duhan was dying. No new companions could replace them in the King's confidence. His affection for his sister Wilhelmina at Bayreuth was as strong as ever but he remained only formally bound in marriage to Elizabeth-Christine and in general showed an antipathy for feminine company. Though making an exaggerated cult of intellectual friendship, Frederick was at heart a lonely and self-tortured man.

It would be a mistake to regard him as a mere psychological freak, a 'crazy mixed-up' king. He possessed an almost Stoic sense of duty, intensified by a desire to achieve greater material success than any previous Hohenzollern ruler. At times he seems to have

Frederick's triumphal entry into Berlin.

93

seen himself as the archetypal eighteenth-century monarch: a prince who despised the trappings of kingship, a warrior leader who won his battles by intuitive unorthodoxy and not by book lessons from the past, and an enlightened lawgiver serving the State through the dictates of reason rather than through sacrosanct authority bestowed by the Church. These were the qualities that won for him warm commendation from the intellectuals of France, who frequently found it profitable to see him as sovereign of their 'republic of letters'. In reality Frederick shared few of their beliefs: he too distrusted clericalism and was interested in speculative thought for its own sake, and he had a wider tolerance of heterodox opinion than most rulers, but ultimately his imperious sense of absolute power imposed a check on his willingness to patronize new ideas. Unlike the writers and thinkers whom he admired, Frederick could no longer stand aside and observe human behaviour with detachment, optimistically convinced of mankind's final perfectability. The 'tranquillity' he had cultivated at Rheinsberg was gone beyond recall. A life of constant action left him with few illusions. The more he saw of war and diplomacy, the more he tended to despise humanity for its folly and stupidity.

Yet Frederick's growing cynicism never destroyed one of his earliest beliefs. He remained convinced that a sovereign had an obligation to his people to encourage sound learning. From the very beginning of his reign he had tried to make the Berlin Academy an international institution, a community of scholars in

An eighteenth-century view of Berlin, showing the Catholic church and the Opera House, for whose company Frederick was to supply libretti.

which non-Germans would enrich the cultural and intellectual life of the Prussian administrative capital while stimulating Frederick's own subjects to interest themselves in science and the humanities. In 1740 Frederick invited to Berlin the distinguished French scientist Pierre-Louis de Maupertuis, who had verified Newtonian theories on the shape of the earth by journeying to the Arctic circle four years previously and measuring there a degree of the meridian. Maupertuis duly came to Berlin but in the following spring he accompanied Frederick to the wars, and was captured by the Austrians on the day of Mollwitz, a misfortune which inclined him to go back to Paris. So long as the Silesian Wars continued, Frederick was unable to keep a close eye on the Academy and was disappointed by the reports which reached him of its activities. In the summer of 1745, however, he persuaded Maupertuis to return and take over the presidency of the Academy. Maupertuis accordingly remained the intellectual leader of Prussia throughout the decade of peace which followed the Silesian Wars. During these years Frederick was pleased to see the Academy grow rapidly in prestige, especially as a centre of the mathematical and scientific disciplines. Philosophy and literature, on the other hand, lagged behind the natural sciences, partly because of the King's insistence that French should be the only language authorized for use in the Academy's proceedings. Although, as Frederick had hoped, this made the Academy's contributions to scholarship available for all the civilized peoples of Europe, it imposed upon his subjects the superfluous impediment of having to express their deepest feelings in an alien language. Frederick's predilection for French was a mixed blessing for Prussia's cultural life.

The King himself sometimes permitted papers he had written to be read to sessions of the Academy. He undoubtedly possessed remarkably wide intellectual and artistic talents, gifts which offset the bleak and almost ascetic austerity of his public life. Rheinsberg had shown his good taste, his instinctive feeling that German Baroque needed the lightening touch of Mediterranean grace. He continued, as King, to enjoy all the visual arts although showing marked prejudices of his own; thus, selected servants despatched to Italy to purchase good paintings, found their task made difficult by his vehement injunction that they were not to bring back 'scoundrel saints undergoing martyrdom', and the exquisite sensitivity to feminine tenderness of the Watteaus and Lancrets in which Frederick delighted is strangely out of keeping with his character. His sense of artistic appreciation was probably less developed than his understanding of music, a childhood enthusiasm which matured with the passage of years. Frederick remained a good flautist and became a competent composer. The simple march with which he sought to celebrate the victory of Hohenfriedberg is still occasionally performed and so indeed is one of his symphonies. When, in 1748, Frederick met Johann Sebastian Bach for the first time, the ageing master of counterpoint was genuinely impressed by the King's understanding of fugal discipline.

Throughout his life Frederick continued to find in literary composition a relaxation second only to music. 'Whenever I have some moments to spare', he once confessed, 'I am seized by a desire to write. I cannot resist this lighthearted pastime which occupies me, diverts me and yet makes me fitter for work.' Some of Frederick's writing was, indeed, 'lighthearted': he had written a short comedy for the wedding festivities of Reyserlingk in 1743 and he enjoyed supplying libretti for the Berlin Opera. He took his writing of poetry more seriously, though in quality it varied considerably for, while his verses were frequently well-turned, endless Alexandrines lauding the primary virtues in stilted French suggested that he was too self-consciously concerned with prosody to be its master. His prose style, on the other hand, was always clear, whether he was giving considered judgements on the nature of warfare or expounding the humanistic philosophies of the Enlightenment. For the most part he subordinated his literary interests to his general conviction that a sound and civilized cultural life demands rational thought, free from religious or narrowly nationalistic prejudice.

Like Clarendon before him and like Churchill and Trotsky in a later century, Frederick wrote passages of political autobiography in which he sought to set off his personal activities against the general context of the age in which he lived. The most ambitious and interesting of his prose compositions is the *Histoire de mon temps*, which began as a frank apologia for the power politics of the Silesian adventure. The first draft was completed as early as 1743 but the King was not entirely satisfied with this rare exercise in the writing of contemporary history and he continued to revise his work throughout the decade of peace. At times it reads as though he had constantly in mind, not only the doubters of his own generation, but the criticisms which would be levelled against him by future historians of diplomacy as well:

I hope [he declared in the original preface] that the posterity for whom I write will distinguish the philosopher in me from the ruler, the man of

honour from the politician. I must confess it is very difficult to maintain purity and good faith if one is caught up in the stormy waters of European politics. One sees oneself constantly in danger of betrayal by one's allies, desertion by one's friends and threatened with humiliation through jealousy and envy. Ultimately one is forced to choose between terrible alternatives, sacrificing either one's people or one's word of honour.

Despite Frederick's apparent candour, the *Histoire de mon temps* remains a work of subtle propaganda, though it is special pleading on behalf of Prussia in Europe rather than for his own reputation. In the two early volumes on the Silesian Wars – and even more in the later ones on the Seven Years' War – Frederick admits he made occasional errors, both as a soldier and a prince. He was proud of his achievements in war and statecraft but not inclined to boast of them. It is this moderation, 'only speaking of myself when I must', which forms the most attractive trait in his autobiographical style.

During the years 1746 and 1747 Frederick was able to give free play to yet another passionate interest in his life. 'Buildings are my dolls', he remarked. Already, at the outset of his reign, he had commissioned Knobelsdorff to add an east wing to his grand-mother's palace at Charlottenburg, which as a home he much preferred to the Royal Palace on the Spree, four and a half miles away in central Berlin; and he had also instructed Knobelsdorff to refurbish the *Stadtschloss* in Potsdam so as to provide him with a happier setting than the drab apartments of Frederick William's reign. But once the Silesian Wars were over Frederick turned to a more grandiose project. He ordered Knobelsdorff to build him an entirely new residence at Potsdam, one where he could lighten the burden of kingly responsibility and seek to re-create the lost dream world of Rheinsberg. A little more than a mile from the *Stadtschloss* there was royal parkland surmounted by a windmill and a steep hill looking out over the town and the River Havel. It was on the summit of this promontory that Knobelsdorff wished to build a new Rheinsberg.

But Frederick wanted a palace which would capture the spirit of Rheinsberg rather than its outward appearance, and he imposed his ideas upon his architect with obstinate determination. The lower slopes of the hill were, on Frederick's orders, terraced and planted with vines. There were, in all, six terraces, each sited meticulously eleven feet above the other and rising from a huge fountain, to be topped by a single storey building, a rambling rococo pavilion strangely unobtrusive amid a cluster of ornamental

OPPOSITE Johann Sebastian Bach, who at the age of sixty-three met Frederick and was impressed with his musical abilities.

A flute concert in progress at Sans Souci.

trees and neatly trimmed hedges. The climate was, of course, far too cold for vines, and the terraces were therefore enclosed within twelve long glasshouses with a broad flight of steps – 144 of them – separating the eastern and western slopes of the hill. In the centre of the south front of the palace was an oval dining room with long glass doors through which the King and his guests could step directly into the garden. The original idea of an artificial vineyard was soon abandoned, although the greenhouses allowed Frederick to cultivate fruit and flowers rarely seen north of the Alps. The beauty of the palace was in part a reflection of its setting amid the richly wooded hills of the Havel lakes, but its charm was accentuated by the elegant symmetry of Knobelsdorff's plan and the good taste with which Frederick countered any suggestion of ostentatious display. Above the portico of the dining room were inscribed

100

the words *Sans Souci* ('Free from Care'), the spirit which the King hoped would always pervade his summer palace.

Sans Souci was ready for occupation before the end of May 1747, and Frederick at once went into residence. His personal apartments were in the east wing of the palace and included a library (with not a German book on its shelves), a bedroom decorated in pastel shades, a music room and a gallery in which were hung some of his favourite pictures, works by Watteau, Pesne and Lancret as well as some of the earlier Flemish painters. Guests were accommodated in the west wing and would be expected to join their host for the main meal of the day at noon as well as passing the evenings with him in conversation or making music. Frederick's favourite sister, Wilhelmina, referred to Sans Souci as 'a monastery' of which her brother was 'the Father Superior'. She alone among women was invited to dine at the palace; indeed it was reported that the only other females seen there were the King's whippet bitches, who rarely left their master's company. Voltaire, who was to spend many months as a guest at Sans Souci, compared the exclusive masculinity of the King's chosen society to Plato's circle of friends in the olive-grove near Athens: 'No woman and no minister of the gospels ever entered Sans Souci', he declared. Yet, with its silk hangings and elaborate ornamentation, the palace was furnished with an essentially feminine delicacy of taste. Nothing could be more different in mood or character from the tobacco-filled rooms of Frederick William's convivial evenings than his son's round table at Sans Souci, where the conversation of host and guests was said to outshine the setting sun on the tiny panes of the glass-covered terraces below them.

But was it really all so brilliant? At times the talk seems to have been as pretentiously over-cultivated as the oranges and figs which the greenhouses protected. Frederick wished to impress his guests with the extent of his knowledge and his good memory: his informal exchanges were in reality elaborate exercises of a promising talent denied full development by the circumstances of kingship. He set the topic of conversation, tossed off pretty phrases lightly spiced with wit, and savoured the *bon mots* of his guests so long as they did not didactically expose the limits of his self-education. Laughter and applause were gratifying, argument prompted mocking repartee but contradiction all too often ended in personal maliciousness. That there was no room at Frederick's table for a pedant is not surprising, but it is hardly to his credit that envy should have led him to humiliate gifted minds more

101

Music in Frederick's Prussia

Frederick was a passionate and
accomplished amateur musician.

LEFT His flute, preserved
today in the Hohenzollern
Museum. ABOVE A solo part
for the flute, written by
Frederick himself. RIGHT A
musical evening in Sans
Souci with Frederick in the
foreground reading his
flute part.

RIGHT Frederick's own plans for the construction of terraces at Sans Souci. BELOW How the terraces looked eighty years later.

emancipated than his own for the sake of his dignity.

This unattractive side of Frederick's personality eventually darkened Voltaire's celebrated visit to Potsdam. Voltaire came to Berlin in June 1750 with a promise of free lodging and a gratifyingly large pension. He was housed in delightful rooms at Sans Souci and encouraged to make constructive comments on the King's historical writings and on his verses. For some months Frederick and his household flattered their distinguished visitor, who was given the office of Chamberlain and the highest decoration in Prussia, the *Pour le Mérite*. But Voltaire, whose letters to Frederick were always heavy-laden with compliments, saw no reason to abase himself at the supper-table. His irony, especially over military matters, irritated the King, who allowed his own misogynistic resentment to prompt him into an unchivalrous attack on the literary aspirations of Voltaire's niece. Ambitious gossips in the small world of Sans Souci were delighted to feed Frederick with some of the least tactful of Voltaire's private asides. The King was not amused. It was bad enough for the Frenchman to regard warfare as a boring topic of conversation when he had the rare privilege of hearing, whenever he wished, the reminiscences of the victor of Hohenfriedberg himself: it was even worse that, on receiving the latest instalment of royal verses for editorial correction, he should have yawned and remarked, 'More dirty linen to be washed . . .!' Before long Voltaire was complaining, in a private letter that, with kings, the phrase 'My dear friend' meant 'You are less than nothing to me' and that the invitation 'Come and sup with me this evening' was a way of saying 'Let me make a fool of you tonight'.

There is no doubt Voltaire behaved unwisely in Berlin. He tried to use inside knowledge to speculate in Saxon state bonds and then publicly quarrelled with the financier to whom he had entrusted the transaction. The King accordingly sent Voltaire away from Potsdam until the storm blew over. Outwardly there was a reconciliation between Frederick and his nominal Chamberlain, who was invited back to the town of Potsdam and the round-table at Sans Souci though no longer accommodated in the palace itself. Their friendship was, however, too artificial to stand the strain of close proximity. Frederick, though eager to keep Voltaire as a tame intellectual at Court, subjected him to petty insults. The great philosopher refused to compromise. When Voltaire believed Maupertuis had acted unjustly towards a Dutch mathematician whose views differed from those of the Frederician establishment,

OVERLEAF A plan of the palace and gardens of Sans Souci.

Orangerie. Lerchen Heide. Pavillon. Weinberg. Der.

Prospect des Königl. Lust Schloßes und

Pavillon   Lerchen Heide.

Bilder Gallerie

Weinberg

weinberg

s Sans soucy, bei Potsdam.

he wrote a caustic pamphlet attacking the President of the Berlin
Academy. Frederick saw this open intervention in German
academic politics as ingratitude, ordered Voltaire's pamphlet to
be burned by the common hangman and wrote an ill-disguised
anonymous reply supporting Maupertuis and intemperately abus-
ing his critics. 'The language', Voltaire commented, 'was French
but the coarseness German.'

Even after this petty and petulant feud, Frederick invited
Voltaire to dine with him nightly for a full week at Sans Souci. But
there were too many others at table eager to discredit the Frenchman for the conversation to be 'free from care'. At the end of
March 1753 Voltaire left Potsdam taking with him the Chamberlain's key of office, the *Pour le Mérite* order, and a slim volume of
Frederick's poems, one at least of which appears to have been
blasphemously obscene. There followed an absurd three-months'
wrangle in which Frederick used his power in German politics to
have Voltaire placed under house arrest at Frankfurt in order to
recover the key, the decoration, and the verses. Inevitably
Frederick had his way. Within two years Voltaire took his revenge
by denigrating his royal friend's character in (of all unlikely places)
the original edition of a mock-heroic poem about Joan of Arc.
Fortunately both men were prepared to forget each other's insults
before the end of the decade and largely through the intervention
of Wilhelmina, they resumed their correspondence. Each recognized that they could cherish their friendship only at a distance.
'I could not live with you, nor without you', wrote Voltaire
cryptically, and Frederick, for his part, complained, 'Voltaire is
the most malevolent madman I have ever met – he is only good to
read'. But by the time Voltaire died, a quarter of a century after his
wretched departure from Potsdam, Frederick had lost all bitterness
towards him. 'I was born much too soon', the King said, 'but I do
not regret it; I have seen Voltaire.'

It would be a mistake to imagine Frederick in these middle years
of his life as a ruler entirely engrossed in the mocking wit and
music-making of a palace 'free from care'. Sans Souci was a unique
place of retreat, the home of a man who had no taste for the normal
relaxations of German princes, but even here Frederick had made
Knobelsdorff include in the plans for the east wing of the palace
an audience chamber where the sovereign could receive ministers
or foreign emissaries whose business could not wait. For Frederick
was resolved never to neglect the tasks of government. When in
residence at Potsdam, he undertook much of the routine adminis-

A statue from Sans Souci.

trative work in the *Stadtschloss* rather than allow it to destroy the serenity of Sans Souci, but at times the sheer accumulated weight of reports and memoranda was so great that they enslaved him in the palace on the hill as well. 'The Prince', he once said, 'is the first servant of the State. If he is well paid for his tasks it is in order that he may maintain the dignity of his office.'

By modern standards, the King had a remarkable number of offices to maintain. He was virtually his own Prime Minister, Foreign Minister, Chancellor of the Exchequer and Minister of Defence, and in 1749 he assumed personal direction of the kingdom's whole economic policy. Frederick William's administrative reforms had centralized authority in the hands of the sovereign although, in internal affairs, he relied heavily upon a 'General Directory' of four ministers. Frederick, however, had little use for ministerial advice. The only time he summoned a council of ministers was when he wished to prepare the annual budget, and even then he resented proposals which ran counter to his preconceived ideas. He did not trust the competence or the judgement of

110

others. Civil servants and departmental heads were, in his eyes,
mere adjutants, whom he expected to transmit his orders and
ensure that his subjects acted upon them. Among his ministers,
only Cocceji, the head of the judiciary, was ever accorded a fair
hearing. Frederick believed in autocratic rule to a dangerously
narrow extent, for the bureaucratic system which he devised could
be operated only by a ruler of his gifts and tremendous energy.
There was little attempt to co-ordinate policy or administration.
Frederick himself was the dynamo which kept the whole governmental machine running day after day. So long as his health was
sound, the machine worked efficiently, but as he grew older and
his vitality began to ebb, the burden became too great for any man
to sustain.

Frederick employed three principal methods of exercising his
personal control. He expected the provincial administrators to
submit long reports on every aspect of their work. If the subject
was of interest to him, he would read it carefully and annotate
it: if not, he would hand it over to one of his three secretaries

The view from Sans Souci of
the city of Potsdam.

111

A party at Rheinsberg, the palace where Frederick had earlier spent much of his time.

whom he had trained to summarize the gist of a document in a few sentences so that he could take rapid decisions on policy. This procedure was, of course, coldly remote from the real problems of the kingdom and Frederick therefore supplemented his paper studies by tours of inspection in each peacetime summer so as to familiarize himself with local difficulties. Finally he relied extensively on a group of special agents (*Fiscals*) who checked the workings of central and local administration and reported directly to the King any instances they encountered of corruption or inefficiency. Frederick's natural cynicism made him, at times, doubt the Fiscals' honesty and he would occasionally intervene himself in comparatively trivial disputes, invariably supporting the claims of any subject who could convince him that he was being unjustly exploited either by the local aristocracy or by servants of the State. The King prided himself on his instinct for recognizing injustice.

The surviving records of Frederick's tours of inspection show that he must frequently have been a tiresome embarrassment to his bailiffs and officials. They had to contend not only with his suspicion of any replies they gave to his questions but also with his obstinate insistence that he knew and understood problems about which he was, at best, superficially acquainted. He tended also to generalize from his experiences as a member of the council of war and agriculture at Küstrin. On the other hand, there is no doubt that his judgement was sound on topics he had studied in his leisure hours as Crown Prince or King. He taught himself to believe wholeheartedly in the virtues of mercantilism although, like every other statesman of eighteenth-century Europe, he had his own idea of precisely what he meant by this fashionable economic doctrine.

In the middle years of his reign, Frederick was as eager to stimulate state economic control of industry as Peter the Great had been in Russia half a century previously. Like Peter, Frederick encouraged industry by attracting skilled immigrants who could train the native population in new techniques and by writing directives of his own on the best ways of production. Sometimes, it must be admitted, hasty reading betrayed itself in royal confusion over technicalities, and the King's personal tastes may have led him to concentrate excessively on the manufacture of luxury goods (although it could be argued that he believed there was a need for Prussia to outshine neighbouring Saxony in this respect). Basically his ideas were sound enough. There was nothing wrong

OPPOSITE Eighteenth-century
crafts: weaving and
spinning in Frederick's day.

with his advice on the spinning of thread or the care with which silkworms should be protected, nor indeed with his instruction for the efficient making of shoelaces. Again and again, in formal documents and private letters, he rammed home the simple message, 'We must spare ourselves the necessity of importing objects we desire from abroad by setting up our own factories here'. Commerce, so he once told his officials, had the prime objective of 'bringing in money from foreign countries' while it was the task of the manufacturers to prevent, so far as possible, any money from leaving the country, and the welfare of the kingdom depended upon a proper relationship between these two functions.

Frederick tended to stress the political character of mercantilism rather more than did the theorists of western Europe. By reducing internal tolls, improving communications and pursuing a unified commercial policy for the kingdom as a whole he hoped the mercantilist doctrines would help to weld together Prussia's widely dispersed territories. This was asking too much of what was essentially an economic doctrine: the differences in social structure and resources between one region and another were so great that it needed more than ten years of peaceful commerce to bring them together. Moreover many aspects of Frederick's policy – high external tariffs, misguided investment in unsuitable enterprises, the stifling of initiative by over-rigid regulations – were already condemned as archaic by the intellectuals of Paris, some of them men who, in other matters, lauded the ruler of Prussia as a champion of enlightened thought. But, in one respect at least, Frederick refused to be a slave of mercantilist dogma: he did not neglect agriculture for the sake of the nascent industries. His fertile mind was attracted by the scientific farming methods already well-advanced in Britain and the Netherlands, and he was constantly seeking to raise the yield of crops and to rationalize the breeding of livestock. These efforts were frustrated, partly by the inherent conservatism of landowners and peasantry, but even more by the ravages of his later campaigns. Unfortunately Frederick seems never to have decided if he wanted swords beaten into plough-shares or pruning-hooks into spears.

In later years Frederick and his admirers came to look back on the decade of peace which followed Hohenfriedberg and the Soor as a lost 'golden age': the King was happy as a hard-working administrator, his leisure hours given over to his verses, his music and the delights of Sans Souci. This, so Prussian historians maintain, was the Frederician Epoch at its best, before the envy of

114

The ravages of war made a massive house-building programme essential in
Frederick's Prussia: bricklayers, carpenters, stonemason and labourers at work.

others forced him to take up arms again so as to preserve the very existence of the kingdom he had brought to maturity. Although it is doubtful if Frederick's intentions in foreign affairs were so peace-loving as this interpretation of history suggests, it remains an attractive piece of nostalgic sentiment. So far as achievements are concerned, it is not without justice. These ten years saw Frederick come closest to his ideal of a modern Renaissance prince, patron of the arts and sciences. There was only one more important building enterprise undertaken in the later period of his reign. The Academy never regained the stature it enjoyed under Maupertuis, nor could Frederick himself recover the social prestige his Court enjoyed at mid-century. Moreover, these were the years in which Frederick's Chief Justice, Samuel von Cocceji, introduced a series of reforms which raised the Prussian judicature to a level of impartiality envied throughout continental Europe and ensured that all the courts of the kingdom followed a common code of legal procedure.

Knobelsdorff, the architect whom Frederick had made a personal friend, died in 1753. Cocceji, the one minister whom Frederick respected, followed him to the grave two years later. It is a sad comment on Frederick's reign that, though the King still had over three decades of life ahead of him, there were no more governmental reforms of lasting significance, nor did any other artistic creation match the charm of the little palace on the hillside above Potsdam.

5 Thunder and Lightning

THE DRESDEN PEACE OF CHRISTMAS 1745 left Prussia in an enviably strong diplomatic position. While the War of the Austrian Succession dragged on for three more years in Italy and the Low Countries (and so far as Britain and France were concerned, in North America and India as well), Frederick, having withdrawn from the contest so early, was able to use his power and prestige as a bargaining counter between the belligerents. Technically he remained an ally of Louis xv but, in the final phases of the war, the British made a determined effort to induce Prussia to join them in curbing French ambitions in the Rhineland and the Netherlands. Frederick, however, was not interested in these areas of Europe at that time. He was courteously unreceptive to the blandishments of the English envoys, although he had every intention of exploiting such rare signs of George ii's goodwill so as to obtain, in the eventual peace negotiations, the one reward he sought for his years of belated neutrality. The Treaty of Aix-la-Chapelle in October 1748 accordingly included among its terms of settlement an international guarantee of Silesia's new frontiers. Eventually it might prove desirable to strengthen Prussia's position in the Polish lands and along the Baltic seaboard, as Frederick had foreseen eighteen years previously in his studies at Küstrin, but for the moment, he was content with his diplomatic success. By the Aix Settlement central and western Europe recognized the finality of his conquest.

Yet within a few months of the Aix treaty Frederick was able to see for himself the illusory character of his achievements. His scant regard for wartime obligations made the political bonds between Potsdam and Versailles tenuously thin while the aloofness which had been an asset in 1747 left Prussia isolated and exposed once the general fighting was at an end. Moreover, there had been a significant change in the pattern of international affairs during the last two years of the war. Russia, sunk into anarchy during the first Silesian campaign because of the sudden death of the Empress Anna, was now again a formidable power. In December 1741, while Frederick's attention was concentrated on the affairs of Bohemia and Moravia, a military revolt in St Petersburg brought to the throne Elizabeth, the younger daughter of Peter the Great. At first Frederick was well disposed towards the new ruler of Russia. She seemed in foreign affairs her father's successor, and it suited Frederick to have the Swedes and Russians once more disputing control of the Gulf of Finland. When, in 1745, Elizabeth married off her nephew and heir-apparent to a daughter of one

PREVIOUS PAGES The Prussians storming a town during the Seven Years' War.

OPPOSITE Elizabeth I of Russia, whom Frederick regarded – quite justifiably – with deep suspicion.

A medallion of Bestouzhev, Elizabeth's scheming and ruthlessly competent Chancellor.

of Frederick's princely army commanders, he was willing to believe that Russian policy would henceforth fall under the influence of Prussia rather than of Austria. This was an illusion, as he soon discovered: the girl (who, in time, became the great Empress Catherine II) was only sixteen years old, and from the moment she arrived in St Petersburg, Elizabeth and her Chancellor Bestouzhev supervised her household so effectively that any lingering partiality she might possess for Prussia was easily suppressed. It is true that Catherine's ineffectual husband Peter (who had been born in Holstein) continued throughout his life to admire Frederick and his policy, but no one in the Russian capital took Peter seriously, least of all the Empress or his wife.

By the winter of 1747-8 Frederick had come to distrust Elizabeth and to see in her ambitions a threat to his own eastern provinces. He knew Bestouzhev was an Austrophile and he regarded the despatch of a Russian army corps to the Netherlands for service against the French as a dangerous portent, even though the war ended before the Russians saw any fighting. He suspected (rightly) that there was a secret alliance between Elizabeth and Maria Theresa, with the Russians undertaking to march westwards into East Prussia should he launch another attack on Bohemia or Moravia. There was no doubt Elizabeth wished to strengthen Russia's hold on Poland and, though Frederick found it hard to believe she would carelessly pit the ill-trained Russian soldiery against his seasoned veterans, he could not ignore attempts by Bestouzhev to provoke a general conflict in the course of 1749. Fortunately for Frederick the crisis of that year evaporated once he began to concentrate his army along the frontiers, but it was clear that his strategic calculations had in future to allow for the simultaneous invasion of his territories from the east and from the south. Moreover, if Austrian diplomacy could encourage the Dutch or the 'Anglo–Hanoverians' to march in the west, there was a strong possibility he might have to wage a defensive war on three fronts, a nightmare prospect. Prussia's exposed geographical position, with no natural barriers to stem an invasion, made it essential for him to anticipate his opponents' moves well in advance. Should the military initiative ever fall from his grasp, he was in danger of losing his scattered provinces one by one.

Frederick, though aware of the danger, remained optimistic. Towards the end of the year 1752 he wrote a long political testament, nominally intended to instruct his successor in his methods of internal administration and the wiles of statecraft. What he

122

wrote on home affairs is painstakingly detailed but predictable: his sections on foreign affairs are, by contrast, remarkably informative both about himself and his policy. For Frederick was concerned to give, not merely an outline of the existing situation, but an assessment of future political projects so that his heirs could determine what were the most desirable territorial acquisitions for Prussia and how they were to be obtained. The revelations of this practical manual of power politics (made public only after the First World War) give a cynical twist to his professions of peaceful intent.

'By our geographical position', he wrote, 'we are neighbours of the mightiest princes in Europe, all of them alike jealous of us and secret enemies.' The most ambitious opponent was Austria, 'of all powers in Europe the one we have most deeply offended, never willing to forget the loss either of Silesia or of that part of her authority in Germany which we now share with her'. Other countries were less of a menace: George II had ambitions, at Prussia's expense, for his Hanoverian possessions; Russia, rather surprisingly, was no more than 'an accidental enemy', whose hostility would disappear once Bestouzhev fell from grace; Saxony was 'a ship without a compass' while the rulers of the Netherlands did not possess 'enough discernment to know whom to love and whom to hate'. Despite these envious neighbours Frederick maintained that Prussia would 'never lack allies', the natural leader of them being France. For the moment, however, the French were weary of fighting: 'My present system is therefore to prolong peace so far as is compatible with the dignity of the State.' If it eventually becomes necessary to go to war there can never be 'another lightning stroke similar to the attack on Silesia' for 'imitations of a masterpiece invariably fall flat'. So long as Russia stands powerfully armed beyond our frontiers 'it is safer to preserve peace, and wait for a more favourable turn of events'.

The good ruler, so Frederick argued, must nevertheless be ready to take advantage of a sudden change in political circumstances so as to acquire lands to which he is entitled, 'through a claim of primary interest'. 'Of all Europe's provinces none would better suit this state than Saxony, the Polish Prussian lands and Swedish Pomerania because all three round off its territories.' Since the most strategically desirable of these provinces was Saxony, Frederick proceeded to outline a military plan for occupying Dresden and advancing along the line of the Elbe before carrying the war into Moravia so as to induce the 'Queen of Hungary' to accept

123

A portrait of Augustus William, Frederick's younger, but not so intelligent, brother.

Prussia's re-drawing of the central European map. Yet 'acquisitions made by the pen are always preferable to those made by the sword', Frederick declared, and he therefore recommended that Polish Prussia and Swedish Pomerania be obtained through negotiation, in the one case by striking successive bargains with rival factions and in the other by claiming Pomerania as a reward for supporting Swedish designs elsewhere in the Baltic region. In his closing paragraph Frederick commended to his successor the virtues of discretion and dissimulation: 'Should the glory of the State oblige you to draw the sword', he concluded in a final flourish of rhetoric, 'then see to it that both thunder and lightning fall upon your enemies at one and the same time'.

Had Frederick died in 1752 or 1753, it is doubtful if his brother Augustus William would have been capable of pursuing so subtle a policy. But Frederick had no reason for anticipating an early death and it is clear that in drawing up the testament he was as much interested in preparing a memorandum for his own use as in drafting a programme of action which his successor would almost certainly ignore. In all these projects there was an element of pipe-dreaming, as Frederick himself admitted. They rested, moreover, on one assumption which was soon shown to be false: the inevitability of perpetual enmity between the rulers of France and Austria, and the consequent need of Louis XV to retain Prussia as his principal ally. Frederick failed to realize that France was becoming more concerned over colonial rivalry with Britain and less interested in what took place beyond the Rhine. When in April 1755 fighting broke out between the English and the French in North America, Frederick was astonished to find that continental Europe seemed, in Versailles, no longer the principal theatre of operations. He suggested that the French should launch a diversionary attack on Hanover or march once more across the familiar battlefields of Flanders and Brabant. Instead, the French coldly suggested that Prussia might appropriately fulfil her obligations as an ally by invading the Electorate of Hanover. With a Russian army mobilized on the frontiers of Poland, Frederick found the prospect of a march westwards singularly unattractive. And when he learned from his agents that the Empress Elizabeth had in August 1755 concluded a treaty with George II by which Russia undertook defensive obligations towards Hanover in return for a subsidy, Frederick was seriously alarmed by what seemed to him a genuine threat of encirclement.

Frederick's diplomacy over the following twelve months was too clever for success. At the beginning of the year 1756 he responded to British suggestions for a mutual guarantee by Britain and Prussia of each other's frontiers, together with an undertaking that both kingdoms would resist the entry of foreign armies into Germany. He believed this 'Convention of Westminster' would safeguard him from a Russian invasion and he could not understand why the French maintained that the treaty was a new instance of his duplicity. The Convention, he argued, was perfectly compatible with the Franco–Prussian Alliance since it neutralized Germany and therefore gave France a free hand to concentrate on the acquisition of territorial gains in the Austrian Netherlands (Belgium) without fear of an attack from across the Rhine. This casuistic reasoning infuriated Louis XV, who already resented the sarcastic witticisms at the expense of Madame de Pompadour with which Frederick was reported to have enlivened his table-talk. Prussian high-handedness inclined the French to listen more sym-

125

pathetically than in earlier years to proposals for a Franco–Austrian Alliance, a project first mooted at Vienna in 1749 by Anton von Kaunitz, who became Maria Theresa's Chancellor in 1753. Hence in May 1756 – only four months after the conclusion of the Convention of Westminster – a treaty was signed at Versailles by which Maria Theresa undertook to remain neutral in the conflict between Britain and France while Louis XV would take no action against any of her possessions. At the same time France and Austria concluded a formal defensive alliance, promising either troops or a subsidy if an attack were made on the other's European territories. The Austrian ambassadors to Paris continued negotiations throughout the summer, hoping to use this limited understanding as the basis of an anti-Prussian coalition.

Secret agents, as well as his regular diplomatic envoys, kept Frederick well informed of what was happening in Paris and St Petersburg and also in the smaller capitals. He was disappointed to find that British influence on Russian policy was slight, and in the early summer there was again a war scare along the Polish frontier. It even seemed likely that Russia would assist Austria and Saxony to launch an attack on Prussia before the autumn. Frederick answered this threat as he had done seven years previously: he mobilized his army, mounted a show of strength in East Prussia and put all the fortresses of Silesia and Brandenburg on a war footing. By the third week in July he could claim a diplomatic victory; his agents informed him there would be no war this year. But at this stage Frederick made a strange miscalculation. He decided to follow up a preventive mobilization with a preventive campaign. He had convinced himself, on the evidence of reports from his spies, that Dresden was the centre of the conspiracy against Prussia. If he struck suddenly at Saxony he would stamp out a dangerous hornets' nest, find in Dresden evidence of the Austro–Russian–Saxon plan to plunge Europe into another war in order to destroy Prussia, and thereby appeal to public sentiment, not only in the uncommitted German states, but in France as well. Twice, during the first four weeks of August, he demanded assurances from Kaunitz that Maria Theresa was not planning to attack his territories either in 1756 or in 1757. Kaunitz, who was eager for Frederick to put himself in the wrong, saw to it that no acceptable response went from Vienna to Berlin; and Frederick walked into the trap. On 29 August, without bothering to declare war, he ordered the Prussian army to cross the frontier of Saxony and march on Dresden. His greed for a province 'of primary interest'

126

to Prussia made him forget the warning he had included in his Political Testament: he was imitating the Silesian masterpiece of 1740.

The invasion of Saxony was an incredible act of folly on the part of Frederick. Militarily he was denied the rapid victory for which he had sought. The city of Dresden fell easily enough to an overwhelming force but the Saxons offered resolute resistance in the hills around Pirna, a natural defensive position eleven miles southeast of Dresden, above the Elbe. By holding out for a month at Pirna, the Saxons prevented Frederick from striking against Bohemia before the coming of winter, thereby destroying any element of surprise in the campaign and giving Maria Theresa and Kaunitz ample time to continue their preparations. Politically, too, the immediate consequences of the Saxon campaign were disappointing. The ruler of Saxony's daughter was married to the Dauphin of France and was a special favourite of Louis XV; she

Madame de Pompadour, mistress of Louis XV. Frederick's sarcastic remarks about her reached the ears of the French King and enraged him.

127

saw to it that her father-in-law heard of every affront and insult, real or imaginary, inflicted by the Prussians on either of her parents. In later years Frederick himself maintained it was her tears which had finally carried France into coalition against him. There was certainly no sign of sympathy at Versailles (or any of the German courts) for poor Prussia, threatened with extinction by a conspiracy of her neighbours. Nor is this surprising, for when Frederick ransacked the Dresden archives, he could find there no useful weapons of propaganda warfare. Indeed such revelations as they contained posed for him a fresh dilemma. The archives showed clearly enough that the arch-conspirator was not Kaunitz or Maria Theresa – and certainly not the wretched Elector of Saxony – but Elizabeth of Russia, whom Frederick still hoped the British might hold in restraint, provided he did not cause fresh offence in St Petersburg by the injudicious publication of secret documents. The *Mémoire Raisonné* which Frederick circulated to the other governments of Europe in order to justify his actions was necessarily so lacking in corroborative evidence that it convinced no one. Even Frederick came to despise the manifesto when he had the opportunity to look back on these events in perspective.

At the time, however, he was given no such respite. The campaigning season in 1756 was comparatively short. Apart from the Saxon resistance at Pirna, Frederick fought only one engagement against the Austrians, a seven-hour affray at Lobositz on 4 October, with each side seeming to hold itself in reserve as though unwilling to risk a decisive battle until their forces had been augmented by fresh levies. But, even if there was little actual fighting, Frederick was fully occupied with the tasks of governing his kingdom and administering Saxony. He spent much of the winter in Dresden, although he made a brief visit to Berlin and undertook a tour of inspection of the Silesian defences. The news was bad throughout the winter months. Maria Theresa and Kaunitz ably exploited the indignation aroused in Europe by Frederick's resort to war. Both the French and the Russians pledged themselves to put large armies into the field, and in the last week of January 1757 the German Diet formally declared Frederick an enemy of all the states within the Empire and proposed to raise an auxiliary force of German troops who would fight against Prussia under the general command of the French. Even the Swedes, anxious to increase their foothold south of the Baltic in Pomerania, joined the coalition against Frederick in March. Should his enemies succeed in coordinating their strategy, he was in danger of encirclement by

OPPOSITE A contemporary print of Frederick embracing the children of Augustus III after capturing Dresden. This scene is more a political manifesto than a display of spontaneous affection.

over twice as many troops as he could ever hope to raise.

At first it seemed that Frederick would have to face this formidable coalition alone and without any assistance from the British, for George II hoped it might be possible to induce Maria Theresa and her allies to respect Hanover's neutrality. But when the French required free passage through Hanover to attack Prussia from the west, George II hastily raised an army of Brunswickers, Hessians and Hanoverians to hold the line of the River Weser under the uninspired command of his son, the Duke of Cumberland, fresh from pacifying the Scottish Highlands after the Jacobite rising. Frederick thought little of his cousin Cumberland's abilities – 'A great ass', he said bluntly – but at least he hoped that, with a member of the royal family commanding an army in Germany, the English Parliament would take some interest in the continental struggle. This view, however, showed a misunderstanding of both the British temperament and the British constitution: the House of Commons felt no obligation towards any German Electorate; and in London itself there had long been a conviction that Hanover was an altar on which English interests were regularly sacrificed. If Frederick sought aid from Britain, he could gain it only on his own merits as a popular idol, the champion of a good cause menaced by the Papists of Austria and France.

In Frederick's army there were indeed regiments in which the Lutheran concept of dutiful obedience was the essence of all military discipline. The peasants accepted the Protestant heritage as readily as they did the Hohenzollern succession, and as often as not they marched to the tune of Martin Luther's own chorales. Frederick's ingrained agnosticism prevented him from treating the war as a crusade: it was, he once wrote 'far too insignificant a matter to interest Providence'. He relied, for purposes of morale, on regional loyalty and on the professional pride of a soldiery who already considered itself superior to any other army in the world. But he was a realist: when the fighting began his army numbered slightly more than 154,000 men, over half of whom had been born outside Prussia. With mercenaries predominating in the supply services and second-line detachments, it was essential for him to see that his troops were well cared for if he wished to check desertions. He therefore paid especial attention to the basic welfare of the rank and file, insisting that they received a regular ration of one pound of beef each week, that every day breadwagons were despatched from the nearest military depot to an army on the march, and that the baggage-train of each regiment contained a

130

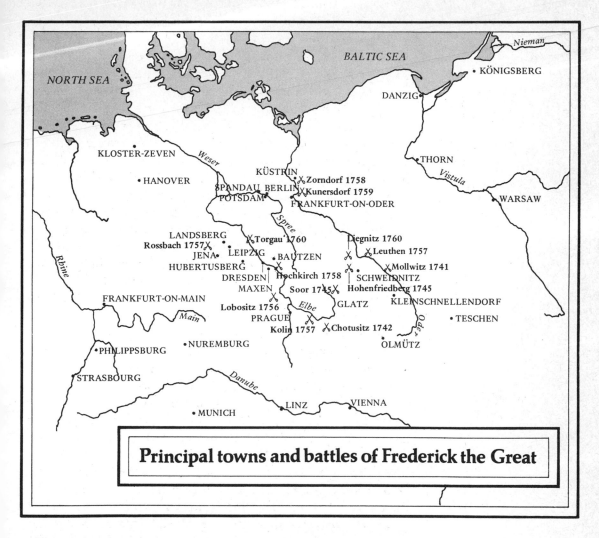

NORTH SEA

BALTIC SEA

Nieman

• KÖNIGSBERG

DANZIG•

KLOSTER-ZEVEN

Weser

•THORN

Vistula

• HANOVER

KÜSTRIN
SPANDAU BERLIN
POTSDAM

✕Zorndorf 1758
✕Kunersdorf 1759
FRANKFURT-ON-ODER

•WARSAW

Spree

LANDSBERG
Rossbach 1757✕
JENA•
HUBERTUSBERG
DRESDEN
MAXEN

✕Torgau 1760
LEIPZIG
•BAUTZEN

Liegnitz 1760
✕Leuthen 1757

✕Mollwitz 1741

Rhine

Hochkirch 1758
Soor 1745✕
Lobositz 1756
PRAGUE
Kolin 1757

SCHWEIDNITZ
Hohenfriedberg 1745
GLATZ
Elbe
✕Chotusitz 1742

KLEINSCHNELLENDORF

• TESCHEN

FRANKFURT-ON-MAIN
Main

OLMÜTZ

Oder

•PHILIPPSBURG
STRASBOURG

• NUREMBURG

Danube

LINZ

VIENNA

• MUNICH

Principal towns and battles of Frederick the Great

sufficient number of pack-horses to carry tents which would protect every single man against the rigours of the weather. What his
armies lost in mobility by these regulations, they gained in discipline and the orderly concentration of manpower at decisive
strategic points in the theatre of war. It was only by harbouring
his limited resources that Frederick could hope to survive the
tempest his invasion of Saxony had raised.

When Frederick visited Berlin at the beginning of 1757, he left
secret instructions that should he be killed or taken prisoner, the
Prussian authorities must continue to wage the war with no
thought of his own fate. For the sake of his sister Wilhelmina he
put on a show of bravado, describing to her in a letter written

OVERLEAF A letter written
by Frederick himself,
containing instructions to his
generals in the event of his
death in battle.

das Corps, das ich bei mir gehabt haben
müßen, die 2 Cürassir Regimenter von
meinem bruder Heinrich laßen, und da lan=
marschiren so gleich wieder nach
Cüstrin nach Franckfort, und so in
der Laußnitz nach dem Laudon inhalt
zu thuen, auf 4 Wochen mußte können
bin aus berlin auf die immer graben
noch trigen, und mit diesem
Corps möglich die Marche deßen
und nach Sachßen marschieren
aufhalten zum Margr: oder Printz
Heinrich Sachßen. und muß gleich
noch immer ist die armée in
meinem Neveus feit gewonnen
Marche und da mein bruder
Heinrich bekommend das Volcken
mit Schwer umbeschreiben officier
ist, so muß die ganze Arme

denen befehle so Respectiren als die
von der Regierenden Herren.

Ich will das nach Meinem Tot Meine
unbekannte mich nicht geärgert werden
mein Tot mich nicht öffnen lassen
Wollen nach sonsaci bringen und
in meinen Garten begraben lassen
daneben ist mein letzter Wille
und haßen das alle Meinen
generale und die Armée Ihre
Stücke noch laden werden
in Lager bei Cüstrin d 22 August 1758

Friderich

N: Solte die bataille verlohren gehen
so muß sich die Armée hinter Cüstrin ziehen
von allen anderen Arméen secure an die
ziehen, und zu versorglichen der Feind von flüchten
wird der auch dahin gehen. F

from Dresden on 5 February how he was saving his strength for the spring, when the Prussians would soon set about the 'motley Austrians, headstrong Frenchmen, wild Russians and those fine fellows from Hungary . . . and silence the impertinent cackling of all that rabble'. But in conference with his commanders he was far less jaunty. Experience, rather than temperament, inclined him to stand on the defensive in order to see which of his enemies made the first probe against his lands. The septuagenarian Schwerin and the enterprising Hans von Winterfeldt (who, in a later age, would have been reckoned his chief-of-staff) proposed a surprise offensive against the Austrian positions in Bohemia, so as to seize the initiative and by destroying their supplies frustrate the long-prepared grand design of the coalition. Frederick modified the details of this plan considerably, concentrating the four invading columns on the single objective of Prague rather than on the whole line of Bohemian fortresses. By the middle of April he was ready to bring the Austrians to battle.

At first the offensive went well. The Austrians had not expected the attack and fell back on Prague, abandoning a large quantity of stores in their precipitate retreat. In Prague they came under the command of Charles of Lorraine who had lost Chotusitz, Hohenfriedberg and Soor in the earlier campaigns. This time, however, the numbers on both sides were far larger: on 6 May, outside the walls of Prague, ninety thousand men were locked in battle – a small figure by the standards of later wars, but three times as many as Frederick was accustomed to seeing engaged in combat. Technically, Frederick won the day and once more defeated Prince Charles, but in the 'bloody battle of Prague' the Prussians came nearer to disaster than in the previous encounters, for Frederick had mistaken a swamp for meadowland and the infantry were caught, floundering in mud and stagnant water, full in the line of fire from the Austrian batteries. Schwerin was killed and Winterfeldt severely wounded. Only a foolish manœuvre late in the day by the Austrian defenders allowed Frederick to drive a wedge in the centre of the enemy line and force Charles to break off the engagement, falling back into the citadel of Prague, which was subjected once again to a siege.

Maria Theresa at once sent from Vienna a relief army under Marshal Daun to take the pressure off Prague. Frederick, seeking as so often in his campaigns to achieve a tactical surprise, advanced to meet Daun and left only a holding force to watch Prague. After a long march, much of it through fields heavy with corn ripening

Con te consumption

Laudat alauda Deum.   oriens ut Lucifer. Iob. 11.

A jubilant Austrian print celebrating Frederick's abandoning of the siege of Prague.

under the midsummer sun, the Prussians found Daun encamped at Kolin, forty miles due east of Prague, on the upper Elbe (18 June 1757). The King allowed his foot-sore veterans three hours rest and then ordered them to launch a flank attack on Daun's positions in the early afternoon. Though suffering heavy casualties, they succeeded in dislodging the defenders from their outposts and Daun had begun the cumbersome task of withdrawing his batteries

LEFT General Schwerin, one of Frederick's aged generals, killed during the battle of Prague.
CENTRE The French army fleeing, with the Prussians in full pursuit at the battle of Rossbach, one of Frederick's most brilliant victories.

RIGHT Frederick visiting a
wounded French general
after the battle of Rossbach.

when one of his cavalry commanders ordered a last, despairing
charge. The Prussian infantry, exhausted, broke and the Austrians,
realizing for the first time that Frederick had already committed
his reserves and that they possessed a numerical advantage, rallied
to the counter-attack. As the light began to fade that evening,
Frederick broke off the engagement and conceded defeat: he had
lost some fourteen thousand officers and men as well as forty-three

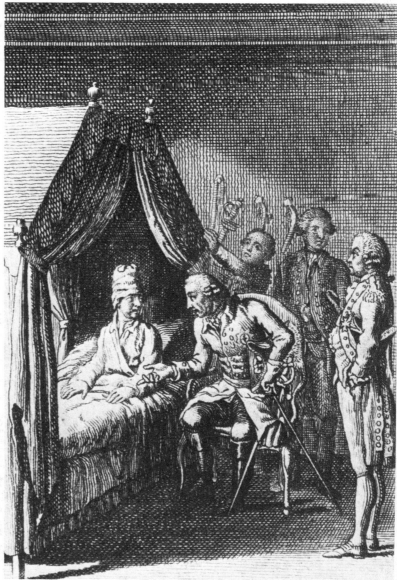

ABOVE Statues on the façade of Sans Souci.

LEFT The façade of Sans Souci.

cannon. His legend of invincibility was shattered and with it, for a time, went his self-confidence.

The four months which followed Kolin were as black as any he had known since the Katte tragedy. He was forced to break off the siege of Prague and the Austrians recovered almost all of Bohemia and much of Silesia. In the west, the French had little difficulty in disposing of Cumberland's army on the Weser, driving it back to the lower Elbe where, at Klosterseven, the Duke signed a humiliating capitulation. There seemed a strong possibility that a Swedish force from Pomerania would link up with the French east of Brunswick and lay siege to Magdeburg. While the Russians advanced into East Prussia on one side of the kingdom, French and Imperial forces mopped up all the outlying Prussian enclaves in western Germany and prepared to march on Dresden. So confused was the situation that in October, a Hungarian column under General Hadik actually penetrated to Berlin and held the capital for three days, exacting a monetary tribute from the civic authorities before it left.

To these political and military tribulations was added a series of personal sorrows. Soon after Kolin Frederick heard that his mother had died, a loss he felt particularly deeply at a time when the glory of his reign was in jeopardy. He was saddened, too, by the incompetent generalship of the heir-apparent, Augustus William, whom he threatened with a court-martial and sent back to his estates in disgrace. When, in the autumn, Winterfeldt was killed in a minor affray in Silesia, Frederick's spirit came near to breaking-point. 'Had I followed my inclination', he confessed to Wilhelmina in mid-September, 'I would have put an end to my life after that wretched battle I lost, but I felt this would be a sign of weakness and that it was my duty to make good the disaster.' So moved was he by the pathos of his predicament that he began each evening to compose French verse: 'I often feel inclined to get drunk and drown my sorrows, but I dislike drinking and the only thing that comforts me is to write verses. As long as I can distract myself in this way, I am oblivious to my misfortune', he explained to his youngest sister on 27 September, enclosing in his letter eighty lines of rhyming couplets on the buffetings of Fortune. He had already written a long and mournful verse-epistle to Wilhelmina, and for his brother Henry he began an ode on Death; but Henry, a phlegmatic soldier, whose vices hardly lent themselves to elegy, was more interested in where the next battle would be fought.

It came on 5 November at Rossbach in Saxony, some twenty

140

miles west of Leipzig. Frederick, whose small army was in danger
of encirclement by the French and Imperial forces under the Prince
de Soubise, suddenly ordered his troops to attack the flank of the
enemy before Soubise had completed his enveloping movement.
It was a brilliant decision which took Soubise completely by surprise. In little more than an hour his army was scattered, isolated
regiments and squadrons seeking the shelter of the Thuringian
Forest or the Harz Mountains with the Prussians, for once, in full
pursuit. The casualties on both sides were astonishingly light for
a battle of such significance. That evening Frederick scribbled a
hurried note to Wilhelmina letting her know the 'good news at
last': 'We have captured all the enemy cannon and their rout is
complete', he wrote, 'Now I can go to the grave in peace because
the reputation and honour of the nation is saved.' In practical
terms he realized the victory gave him freedom of movement, the
opportunity (as he later put it) 'to go and look for new dangers in
Silesia'.

Four weeks later he was face to face with the Austrian enemy
over two hundred miles to the east of Rossbach. For while Frederick
was disposing of Soubise's army, his old antagonist, Charles of
Lorraine, had taken Breslau and much of Silesia, too. Once again
the Prussians were outnumbered, for whereas Charles had sixty
thousand men at Breslau, Frederick's army was no more than
forty thousand. This time the King prepared for battle with more
deliberation than in earlier encounters: he gave instructions as
to what should be done were he to perish, like Gustavus Adolphus,
on the field, and he summoned his senior officers for an unchar-
acteristic eve-of-battle exhortation, which deeply impressed them.
He even wandered round the encampment, talking familiarly with
the rank and file, so eager was he to boost morale to its highest
point. And yet, with all this preparation, he was patient enough
to postpone the assault for twenty-four hours when he saw Charles
bringing his men forward from their fortified positions and preparing to give open battle around the village of Leuthen. 'The fox
has come out of its earth', he declared contentedly as he watched
the enemy movement. He knew the terrain well from peacetime
exercises; and after Rossbach he was once more confident of
victory.

Half a century later Napoleon held Leuthen to be the supreme
vindication of Frederick's generalship. The battle took place on
5 December 1757 (the corresponding week of the year to Auster-
litz). There were only six hours of daylight in Silesia, and Frederick

141

A. Se. Maj. der König von Preussen comandiren den rechten Flugel Berc Armee. B. Fürst Moritz von Anhalt. C. General
Retzow, so den linken Flugel comandiret. D. General Ziethen, so die Cavallerie comandiret. E. 4 Regimenter Preuss In-
fanterie, so anfänglich hinter die Cavallerie des rechten Flügels gestanden, u. selbigen unterstützet. F. der Oesterreichis:
linke Flügel woselbst sich der General Nadasti mit seinem Corps de Reserve befand, welcher gleich anfangs auf die Preuss.
Cavallerie losging, aber bald zurück getrieben wurde, u. völlig in die Flucht sich begiebt. G. Pr. Carl v. Lottringen. H. Gen. Daun.
I. Oest: rechter Flügel, so mit starken Batterien u. Verhacken bevestiget war. K. Gräben, worin Panduren gelegen. L. das
rf Borne. M. das Dorf Leuthen, welches von allen Seiten mit Redouten u. Verschanzungen umgeben war hier währete das
gsechte eine gute Stunde, da die tapfern Preuss Batt: einen Angriff nach den andern wagten, u doch endlich Meister da:
von werden. Die Eroberung dieses Dorfs entschied auch das Treffen, u. es ergriff so wol die feindl Infanterie als Caval: in
gröster Eilfertigkeit die Flucht, u. wurden von der Preuss. Cav. u. besonders von den tapfern Husaren bis in die sin-
kende Nacht verfolget, eine unzählige Menge darnieder gehauen, u. viele 1000 Gefangene eingebracht. N Oesterr.
Bagage u. Munitions Wagen, deren der General von Ziethen den 8ten schon an 3000, nebst der sämtl Bagage
u. den mehrsten Zelten gehabt, und stunden noch alle Wege u. Felder voll. auf den Vorgrund O. ist der Angriff der 4. Sächs. Regimenter leichte Reuter abgebildet. Sonst ist noch erbeutet worden, an 200 Canonen
an 60 Fahnen u. Standarten, u. an Gefangenen hat man Abends den 7ten schon 12.500. gehabt. Der Oester:
Verlust an Todten, die auf dem Platz geblieben, erstreckt sich an 6000 haben
und die Menge der Blessirten noch viel höher. Der
Preuss. Verlust an Todten u. Blessirten wird überhaupt nicht
über 4000 Mann betragen.

142

exploited both the poor visibility and the unusual length of the Austrian line, four and a half miles from one flank to the other. With Charles uncertain of Frederick's intentions, the main Prussian force then moved its line of approach under cover of sloping ground and trees until Frederick was able to bring the whole weight of his attack against Prince Charles's left wing in depth. The Austrian centre, around the village of Leuthen, held out until the late afternoon but it could not resist the pressure on its flanks. The Prussian tactics so confused the Austrians that it was impossible for them to make an orderly withdrawal. In the chaos Frederick was able to take some thirteen thousand prisoners, and within a few days, not only Breslau but the whole of Silesia as well, were clear of Austrian troops. Kolin was triumphantly avenged and Frederick's dominions saved from imminent disaster. That December night the sound of Martin Luther's great hymn of thanksgiving was heard swelling in volume from the tents of the Prussian army until it seemed as if the only man silent and asleep was the King himself, physically and mentally exhausted.

A view of the battle of Leuthen. This victory was later hailed by Napoleon as the supreme vindication of Frederick's generalship.

DVO fulmina

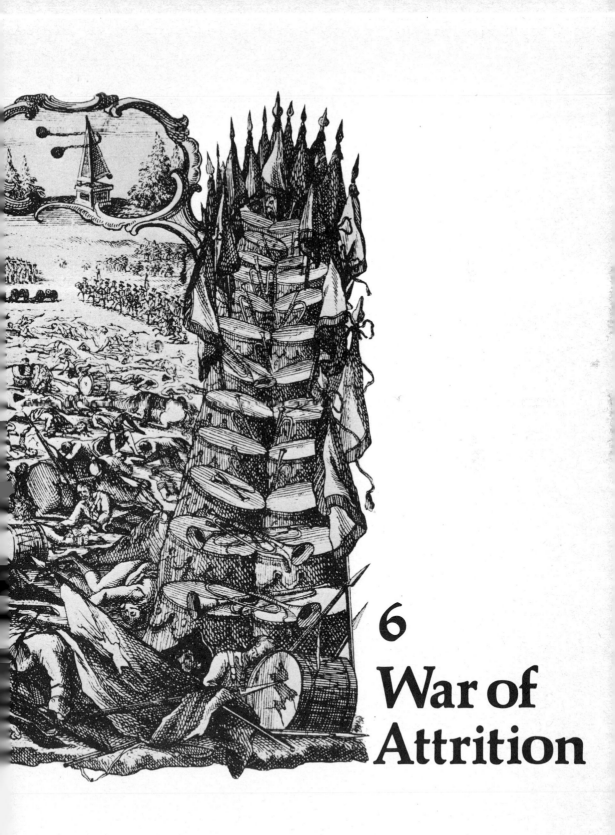

6
War of
Attrition

THE TWIN VICTORIES OF ROSSBACH AND LEUTHEN not only restored Frederick's reputation among his own people: they made him the idol of his English ally. As yet, the Seven Years' War had failed to produce any remarkable triumphs of arms by George II's seamen or soldiers, and in their absence it was heartening to find on the continent at least one champion of the Protestant cause. The Londoners duly rejoiced at their discovery that winter: George Whitefield, the great Methodist preacher, drew a good crowd to his special service of thanksgiving for the defeat of the Papist armies; manufacturers decorated teapots and beer-mugs with what were said to be the King of Prussia's features; taverns and coaching-inns were named after him, not only in London but in Oxfordshire and the western counties as well; and on 24 January his birthday was celebrated rowdily in the capital and in several provincial cities. More significantly, William Pitt (who, as Secretary of State, was the dominant figure in the Duke of Newcastle's administration) saw in Frederick an ally worth sustaining in the field both with subsidies and by the despatch to the continent of English troops. Until Rossbach, Pitt, whose grand strategy was oceanic rather than European in concept, had tended to regard all German entanglements with suspicion, but so long as Frederick was prepared to engage the French in battle, Pitt was willing to identify Prussia's fight for survival with England's endless naval war against Louis XV's colonial empire.

Frederick treated reports of his popularity in England with his customary wry cynicism. He suspected that the Whigs who illuminated their townhouses in honour of the Protestant hero were more concerned with the future of the fur trade in North America and the sugar islands of the West Indies than with the fate of his own scattered dominions. This, of course, was perfectly true and Frederick had no intention of prolonging a terrible continental campaign for the sake of the City merchants in London. He was understandably reluctant to accept any subsidy from Pitt. Provided he could obtain adequate territorial gains – in Saxony, perhaps, or in Polish Prussia – he would rather have ended the war entirely than become an English pensionary. With the French and the Austrians chastened by the two staggering blows of Rossbach and Leuthen, it seemed that he might indeed be able to secure a good peace that winter. He wrote an arrogant, and somewhat incoherent, letter from Breslau to the 'Queen of Hungary' suggesting that 'means be found for settling our differences', and he summoned his friends to Breslau so that they might amuse

PREVIOUS PAGES An eighteenth-century print which shows the Russian general Saltykov and the Austrian general Laudon embracing each other after their joint victory over Frederick in 1759, at Kunersdorf, one of the most murderous battles of the Seven Years' War.

146

William Pitt, Secretary of State, who harnessed English public opinion to regard Frederick as a Protestant hero, and helped him with subsidies and troops. As long as Frederick was fighting the French, he was helping England.

themselves by making music through January and February while awaiting a response from Vienna or Versailles. The King was in good spirits and he was especially pleased with the company of a thirty-three-year-old Swiss, Henri de Catt, who joined him in Breslau as his official Reader and kept a detailed journal of his daily life for the following five years.

Despite Frederick's hopes for peace, no diplomatic initiative broke the silence of Silesia that winter. Though both the Austrians and the French were weary of the German war, the Russians were only now preparing to intervene on a massive scale, their earlier incursion into East Prussia having come to a halt largely through problems of supply. With the Empress Elizabeth informing the French and Austrian ambassadors in St Petersburg that her armies would march on Berlin itself once the summer came, there was no real prospect of an early end to the war. Maria Theresa dismissed Charles of Lorraine at last, replacing him as commander of her forces by Marshal Daun, the victor of Kolin. She also gave high commands in the field to two other enterprising soldiers of fortune, General Gideon von Laudon and Count Lacy, both of them men who had studied dispassionately the lessons of the recent campaign. It would not be so easy for Frederick to outmanœuvre the Daun–Laudon–Lacy combination.

By the beginning of March 1758, Frederick was reluctantly preparing for another summer of marching from one threatened sector of his frontiers to the next. He discounted any immediate danger from Russia, preferring as in earlier years to strike first at the Austrians so as to forestall any offensive they might launch against his positions in Silesia. But he knew that, if the war was to continue, he needed to be certain of British help. Accordingly in April he at last accepted from Pitt an annual subsidy of £675,000, together with the promise of a new Anglo–Hanoverian army on the Elbe, which this time would be commanded not by the incompetent Cumberland but by Frederick's brother-in-law, the young and resourceful Prince Ferdinand of Brunswick. The agreement with the British limited Frederick's freedom of initiative in diplomacy – for Pitt made it clear there would be no money if the King indulged in one-sided negotiations with the enemy – but at least it protected the line of the Elbe, safeguarding the western frontiers of Brandenburg and allowing Frederick to concentrate on the threats from the south and the east.

Frederick's spring campaign of 1758 had, on paper, a familiar appearance. He intended to besiege the city of Olmütz in Moravia, draw the Austrians into battle among the low hills to the south of the town, and, after defeating them, march southwards on Vienna itself. The Prussian army met little resistance as it advanced on Olmütz and by the beginning of May the city was surrounded and subjected to the customary strain of a siege. Daun, who had expected Frederick to invade Bohemia rather than Moravia, advanced with a relief army and then took up a strong defensive position two marching days south-west of Olmütz, waiting for Frederick to attack him as he had done at Kolin. But Frederick was not going to make the mistake of pitting tired troops once more against an enemy who would not come into the open; he too was prepared to wait, confident that Olmütz would fall once the beleaguered citadel ran out of supplies and water. It was a strange situation. While in western Germany Ferdinand of Brunswick's composite army was driving the French back from the Elbe across Westphalia to the Rhine, the Moravian campaign seemed in a position of stalemate. At first, Frederick was patient enough: Henri de Catt describes one evening during the siege when the King could think of nothing better to do with himself than show his prowess as a dancer, following up five or six *entrechats* with a lesson on the intricacies of the minuet. But time was on the side of the Austrians rather than of the Prussians: every week of the futile siege allowed Elizabeth of Russia to mass more and more troops in East Prussia, and by the start of June Frederick was realizing that he could not remain indefinitely in Moravia, with a Russian threat gathering east of Berlin. For a

Marshal Daun, Maria Theresa's enterprising and highly professional new commander, who was to thoroughly frustrate Frederick.

ABOVE Frederick and Voltaire in the colonnade of Sans Souci.

RIGHT Frederick's triumphal entry into Berlin after the peace of Hubertusburg.

mper honos, nomenque tuum laudesque manebunt.
Virg. Ecleg. V.

FREDERICUS REX
...ssburg erfochten Frieden
...Mertz

BORUSSIA Elector Brandeburg.
Friderici post pacem Hubertiburgicam factam 1763. d. 15. Febr. in
Urbem suam Berolinum d. 30 Mart. desideratus reditus.

Rex redit et copias reducit. Date lilia plenis,
Ferte rosas calathis! lætam Rex tendit in Urbem
Iam tuba, Martis opus, taceat: jam cantet avena.
Iam redit dulcis numero plaudente Poesia
Desertus reddat Regem sapientia lucis
Corda tuæ tibi sola ferunt ardentia terræ
Stat Mercator amans lucri sacer Ordo Senatus,
Opifices cumque his defuncti munere belli
Quos pater ut teneros natos curatque fovetque
Turba animosa ruit, pueri vunuptæque puellæ
Sedibus excitæ pensa imperfecta relinquunt.
Immolasque oculos arrectasque auribus adstant.
Salve deliciæ! salve populique voluptas!
Bella valere tube, pacemque amplectere totus.

EX
Bibl. Reg.
Berol.

whole hour Frederick poured abuse on Colonel Balbi, whose sappers had failed to find a way of destroying the Olmütz fortifications. Then news came that Laudon had ambushed a convoy of four thousand wagons loaded with grain and ammunition: now it was the besiegers and not the besieged who were running out of supplies. In the third week of June Frederick disengaged his army, falling back first to Bohemia and then to Silesia, abandoning the summer campaign without once fighting a set-piece battle. None of Frederick's contemporaries understood the art of strategic procrastination so well as Daun, and the honours that summer rested with him rather than with the Prussians.

This frustrating experience depressed Frederick. His mood was made blacker still by news of the death of his eldest brother and heir, Augustus William, with whom he had quarrelled after Kolin. Catt found Frederick unpredictable, sometimes in tears over his

General Laudon blows up Frederick's supplies during the siege of Olmütz.

misfortunes, sometimes content to play for an hour or more on the flute, sometimes declaiming Racine with inspired emendations, and always ready to forget the realities of a long campaign in good conversation about poetry and music. Yet, as Catt soon perceived, the challenge of having to face more than one enemy at a time came almost as a tonic to Frederick. After the rebuff at Olmütz, he consoled himself with the thought that at least he could now attend to the Russians, who had begun to penetrate deeply into Brandenburg.

With astonishing rapidity Frederick marched northwards at the head of some fourteen thousand men until he met the Russian invaders in a part of his kingdom which he knew intimately, the bare plain around the confluence of the rivers Oder and Warthe, dominated by the fortress of Küstrin, of sad memories. Although the Russian commander, Fermor, had nearly twice as many men, the King was confident of victory: he despised the Russian infantry as a horde of serfs and criminals, and it was inconceivable to him that he should fail against such troops in a countryside where he knew every stream, every bridge and every mill for miles around. He planned to attack the Russians at Zorndorf, four miles north of Küstrin, where he hoped his cavalry would drive them, broken, into the Oder. Catt has left an intriguing record of the King on the eve of battle busily writing French verses 'in a very small room in a mill', breaking off to give his generals instructions for the next day and then returning to finish off the verses (and also some grapes). He slept soundly, quite certain that tomorrow the Russians would be sent reeling back across the Polish plains by his grenadiers.

But the battle of Zorndorf (25 August 1758) did not go according to plan. Fermor's army was better disciplined than Frederick had anticipated. Although the initial Prussian attack threw the Russians back, their line held fast against all later onslaughts. Moreover, when Frederick attempted to outflank Fermor, the Russians responded by a counter attack against the opposing flank, so that the two armies reversed their positions while seeking to outflank each other. After ten hours of fighting, the Russians still remained on the field and even resumed the battle next morning, but Fermor knew he could not hope to seize Küstrin and its citadel with a force already badly mauled in the previous day's encounter, and on the night of 26 August the Russians withdrew to Landsberg, twenty-five miles away on a plateau above the Warthe. Frederick had not the strength to

As the wolves of Austria and Hungary were closing for the kill, the worry
lines on Frederick's face grew deeper: Frederick with his generals.

pursue them. Technically he rated Zorndorf as a victory, for the Russians did not risk another assault on Brandenburg for a whole year; but Zorndorf cost the Prussians heavy casualties they could not afford. Frederick was sadly conscious that, while Russia's reserves were virtually unlimited, some of his own better regiments were becoming short of officers and deficient in training. The prospect was bleak. 'I may tell you in confidence,' Frederick remarked to Henri de Catt, 'that the affairs of the State are not desperate at present but my heart is heavy with despair. If only you could see into its depths!'

Within seven weeks of Zorndorf, worse followed. While Frederick was in Brandenburg he left his brother Henry to defend Saxony against Marshal Daun who, in the King's absence, sought to surprise and capture Dresden. Henry was able to check Daun's advance but, with his limited numbers, he dared not risk a battle: better far to leave that to Frederick. But, to the King's indignation, as soon as he arrived back from Zorndorf the Austrians withdrew to the high land along the borders of Bohemia. 'Anyone would imagine Austria recruited her generals in the Caucasus or the Cordilleras', Frederick complained, 'No sooner do they see a mountain top than they climb up it.' The best he could hope for was a feigned withdrawal eastwards, tempting Daun into the plains as he marched towards the upper Spree and the upper Neisse. Against the advice of his most experienced commanders, Frederick halted at the village of Hochkirch, forty miles east of Dresden and about a hundred miles west of Breslau. From the heights above the town Frederick could see the Austrians following him: he did not believe there was any likelihood of an imminent attack, least of all one launched during the long dark nights, for Daun was too conventional a commander to gamble on such an enterprise. The Prussian army was spread out along a series of low hills southwards from the village of Hochkirch, which was itself protected by a redoubt. The length of the Prussian line suggests that Frederick intended to turn against Daun on the first day of good weather, seeking to envelop him from the right.

But Daun did not wait to be attacked. Laudon encouraged him to take advantage of the darkness and autumnal mists. About three-thirty in the morning of 14 October the King's bodyguard, encamped around the centre of the Prussian line, were surprised to hear musket fire away to their right, above the village of Hochkirch. Frederick himself awoke, walked along the front of the tents, listened to the sound of firing and confidently told his

officers, 'That is only a patrol of pandours out on a raid!' But before the King could return to his quarters, cannon shot began falling on the camp: the Austrians had gained a foothold in the village of Hochkirch and brought their own batteries up, under cover of darkness, to the great redoubt. Frederick was thus faced with the engagement for which, under different circumstances, he had so long sought. His guards and cavalry fought for more than seven hours in an effort to dislodge Daun, but they could make no impression on the Austrians. From Hochkirch the enemy batteries were able to fire at point-blank range: Frederick's personal bodyguard suffered heavy casualties and his own horse, 'a magnificent light brown charger', was hit and killed beneath him. By noon there was nothing Frederick could do except extricate the survivors and reform them in a stronger defensive position. This difficult manœuvre he conducted admirably, falling back north-westwards to natural defences around the walled town of Bautzen. Daun did not dare press home his advantage in numbers and material and the orderly withdrawal saved Prussia from any loss of territory, but in Vienna Hochkirch was celebrated as a considerable victory. And rightly so.

Frederick lost more than a quarter of his army (including a third

Typical cannons used to defend a besieged castle during the Seven Years' War.

of his infantry) and over a hundred guns during the seven- or eight-hour engagement. Hochkirch was thus a far more serious defeat for him than Kolin, and some of the younger officers did not spare him their criticisms. Contempt for the accepted rules of warfare is genius when (as at Soor, Rossbach and Leuthen) it succeeds, but at Hochkirch it had seemed in Frederick no more than arrogant folly, an unwillingness to take counsel from his generals or even believe the evidence of his own ears. For the remainder of the war years there was a feeling among the professionals of the Officer Corps that Prince Henry, a meticulously precise commander and an able administrator, had a better understanding than his brother of their needs and problems. Strict discipline and an ingrained habit of obedience preserved their loyalty to the King, but it did not warm their hearts to him.

After Kolin, Frederick's nerve had broken, but this time he was resolved to hold the army together by his own efforts, and he continued to prepare for another encounter with Daun before the onset of winter. 'A great misfortune has, indeed, befallen me', he wrote to Henry on the day following the battle of Hochkirch, 'but with firmness and courage it can be righted.' Yet within forty-eight hours his fortitude was shattered: early on 17 October he

157

OPPOSITE A sketch of
Frederick's brother, Prince
Henry: a dependable and
practical man, much more
straightforward than
Frederick, but unable to see
through the complexities of
foreign diplomacy.

was awakened by the arrival of a courier with news that his sister
Wilhelmina had died on the very day of Hochkirch. The loss of
this one friend from his childhood left him wretchedly alone. For
four days he shut himself up in a darkened room of his quarters
near Bautzen, refusing to see anyone except Catt, to whom he
seemed at times wildly incoherent with grief. At this crisis of his
personal life the Stoicism on which he modelled his conduct,
failed him, as he later admitted. He turned, for the first time in
many years, to theological studies; he began to talk seriously to
Catt about the problems of immortality, the nature of the Last
Judgement, the reality of God – 'If we do not believe in Providence,
how can anything be explained?' he asked. On 20 October Prince
Henry arrived and induced Frederick once again to take up the
burden of work. But for weeks on end the King found it impossible
to sleep. By the middle of November he was frail and feverish, 'as
slow as old Nestor, only fit to be thrown to the dogs', as he himself
wrote. He could hardly stay in the saddle and when at last the
winter snows put an end to all immediate prospects of campaigning, he returned thankfully to the Silesian capital, where for three
weeks he did not even venture outside the walls of his residence.
The year 1758, which had begun so promisingly at Breslau in the
afterglow of victory, ended dismally in the same city with the
King declaiming to himself scene after scene from Racine's
tragedies.

There had been a moment briefly in the autumn when Frederick
believed that the influence of peace parties in both Versailles and
Vienna would enable the war to be ended that year. But in December the Duc de Choiseul became foreign minister of France, giving
Louis XV a war leader as determined as Pitt across the Channel,
and Kaunitz's position in Vienna was never seriously challenged.
By February 1759 Frederick was once more deep in plans for the
new campaign. This time, however, he was forced to acknowledge
Prussia's weakness. With his army reduced to less than a hundred
thousand men and his financial resources severely strained despite
the English subsidy and debasement of the coinage, Frederick
gave up any hope of mounting an offensive. He resolved to await
a move by the enemy and trust that he would be able to snatch
victory in the field. There was little real prospect now that Prussia
would impose her peace terms on Europe: the best he could
expect was a compromise settlement, restoring the frontier which
had existed before his rash invasion of Saxony precipitated war
on the continent. To achieve even this limited success the Prussian

158

kingdom would have to show greater powers of resilience and survival than her neighbours. The conflict had become a war of attrition which would be resolved, not by some startling triumph of arms, but by the ability of one side to continue to win local engagements until the enemy was too short of troops and resources to pursue the struggle. A dispassionate observer in the spring of 1759 would, on this count, have rated Frederick's chances poorly: his enemies could muster more than twice as many men as Prussia, and the rolling plains of his kingdom remained dangerously exposed to marauding invaders.

Strategically the most serious danger for Frederick lay in a union of the Austrian and Russian armies. Daun was content to remain inactive for months on end apart from minor skirmishes, but Laudon (who had served in the Russian army for several years, spoke the language, and looked upon its officers as brothers-in-arms) was eager to join forces with the Russians under their new commander, General Saltykov. In August Daun sent Laudon with a detached Austrian corps to support the Russians in eastern Brandenburg. This was too grave a threat for Frederick to ignore. Once again he left the southern sector of operations and hurried northwards towards Frankfurt-on-Oder with a force of fifty thousand men. On 12 August he encountered the combined Russo–Austrian army at Kunersdorf, six miles east of Frankfurt. He at first attacked Saltykov's left flank and overran it, capturing more than sixty cannon. But when he sought to follow up his initial advantage he found the Russians could not be prised out of their prepared defences and his infantry were exposed to savage cavalry attacks from Laudon's Hussars. Frederick ordered the Prussian artillery forward but the guns stuck fast in the sandy soil. By the end of the afternoon it was clear the Prussians would never break through: the most that Frederick could hope was to retire on Frankfurt in good order.

But this was impossible: defeat became disaster when Cossack horsemen galloped down on the floundering Prussians. Frederick himself was nearly captured. Two horses were killed under him, as he tried to rally the Prussian infantry. A stray shot shattered a snuff box in his pocket. 'Won't some accursed bullet finish me off?', he was heard to cry, as his army fled towards the Oder bridges. But he was denied the glory of dying at the head of his troops. He had to suffer the bitter pain of an overwhelming defeat.

That night Frederick wrote a despairing note to Karl von Finckenstein, the chief minister resident in Berlin: 'My coat is

OPPOSITE An Austrian cavalry attack during the Seven Years' War: ruthless, efficient and deadly.

161

The battle of Liegnitz, where, through a brilliant piece of deception, Frederick was able to escape from a trap and inflict ten thousand casualties on the Austrians.

163

riddled with bullets but, to my misfortune, I am still alive . . . I no longer have my men under control. You would be well advised to look to your safety in Berlin. I have no resources left. To tell the truth, I think all is lost. I shall not survive the destruction of my homeland. Farewell for ever.' He ordered Prince Henry to take supreme command of the army, insisting that the troops should take an oath of loyalty to the new heir to the throne, his fifteen-year-old nephew Frederick William. The King was certain that this time the enemy would advance in strength on Berlin, barely fifty miles west of the Oder, and force the ruler of Prussia to sue for peace.

Saltykov, however, hesitated. His own casualties had been heavy; he was still afraid of Frederick, awed by his reputation rather than by any concentration of arms, and he disliked and distrusted Laudon. 'Another victory as costly as Kunersdorf', Saltykov told the Empress, 'and I alone will be left to bring news of it to St Petersburg'. To Frederick's relief the Russians retired to Poland. At once the King ordered what was left of his army to face southwards and head again for Saxony, for in his absence Daun had at last surprised the weak garrison of Dresden and seized the city. While General Finck was sent ahead with fifteen thousand men to cut off Daun's retreat, Frederick put out peace feelers to Choiseul, using Voltaire as an intermediary. That summer and autumn the French were hard-pressed: they were defeated by Ferdinand of Brunswick at Minden; they had to surrender two of the richest sugar islands in the West Indies and finally they lost Canada with the capture of Quebec in September. There might have been a reasonable prospect of a negotiated peace had not Frederick now completed the ruin of his prestige by bungling the new expedition to Saxony, for inexplicably Finck's force was ambushed by Daun at Maxen, losing ten thousand men (including eight generals) and all their equipment. Prince Henry maintained that Finck should never have been sent on such a mission with battle-weary troops. Even in England there was ironical talk among the Tories of persuading Frederick to go to the Americas, become 'Lord of the Ohio', and exercise his military talents on the Indians. None of the great Westminster houses were illuminated in honour of his birthday that winter.

The war dragged on in Europe as overseas. Choiseul did indeed show less interest in continental campaigns than before Minden, but the two Empresses (Maria Theresa and Elizabeth) tightened their bonds by a new treaty in March 1760 by which it was agreed that Russia should annex East Prussia when Frederick was finally defeated, provided that the Austrians recovered Silesia and Glatz. But – to his own surprise – Frederick staved off defeat throughout the spring and summer campaigns by skilful manœuvring. At Liegnitz in Silesia, forty miles west of Breslau, Frederick was nearly trapped in the second week of August by the Austrian armies of Daun, Laudon and Lacy, but by inducing the Austrians to attack a simulated and empty camp he was able to take Laudon by surprise on the flank and inflict ten thousand casualties. Twelve weeks later Frederick gained an even more impressive victory against Daun at Torgau, on the Elbe north-east of Leipzig. On this occasion he confused Daun (who had, as usual, chosen an excellent defensive position) by attacking simultaneously from north and south while developing the main assault from an enveloping move-ment that appeared to counter-march almost in a semicircle around the Austrian right flank. The victory of Torgau enabled Frederick to recover all of Saxony except for the city of Dresden itself which Daun held for the remainder of the war, despite severe bombard-ment from the Prussian guns. Torgau bolstered up Frederick's waning prestige among his allies, although the weakness of his position was emphasized by a temporary Austro–Russian occupa-tion of Berlin while he was preparing his Saxon offensive.

The strain of the war was so great that Frederick resolved to avoid battles as far as possible throughout the year 1761, hoping that he might be able to weaken the coalition against him by stirring up the Turks, who would attack Russia and Austria from the south. It seemed, in the late summer of 1761, as if the combined Russo–Austrian armies would bring Frederick to battle in Silesia, but the King ordered the construction of a massive series of forti-fications thirty miles south-west of Breslau around the village of Bunzelwitz in the northern foothills of the Sudeten mountains. He retired into the encampment with fifty thousand men and withstood a nine weeks' siege, counting (rightly) on growing tension between his Russian and Austrian enemies. But though this device succeeded, Frederick was deeply conscious of losing the war of attrition. That winter, for the first time, the Russians and the Austrians set up headquarters in occupied Prussian territory. The noose was so tight around Frederick in the closing weeks of 1761 that he admitted nothing short of a miracle would save him. Since he believed that the Age of Miracles was over, he began to accept in his private letters the probability of defeat. Once more he hinted at suicide.

OPPOSITE Peter III of Russia, a passionate admirer of Frederick, who came to the throne just in time to save Frederick from destruction at the hands of the Russians.

But the New Year opened, if not with a miracle, at least with astonishing news from St Petersburg. The Empress Elizabeth, for many years virtually an alcoholic, finally drank herself to death on the Russian Christmas Day. Her nephew and successor, Tsar Peter III, had never disguised his admiration for Frederick. Within hours of his accession he sent an emissary to the King and ordered all military operations by the Russian army to cease. By the spring the Tsar had withdrawn his troops from every tract of Frederick's territory, and the diplomats were busy drafting a new treaty by which the Russians would assist Frederick to throw the Austrians out of Silesia in return for Prussian support in a new war against Denmark. Frederick was so elated by this latest diplomatic revolution that he began to sketch out a grand design for encompassing Maria Theresa's dominions: the Russians would cross the Carpathians, the Turks ravage the Hungarian Plain and the Prussians advance through Moravia on Vienna. With Tsar Peter publicly kissing a marble bust of Frederick in the Winter Palace and kneeling reverently before his portrait, it seemed to the King that Berlin and St Petersburg between them would settle the frontiers of the new map of eastern and central Europe. Already there was friction between Prussia and Britain, where the accession of the young George III had led in October 1761 to the replacement of Pitt by Bute, who was determined on peace and urged Frederick to secure the best terms possible from Austria and give up the thought of further campaigning on an English subsidy. A Russian alliance would more than compensate for what Frederick insisted on regarding as Bute's treachery.

Yet, as Frederick in his calmer moments should have foreseen, there was never any possibility of the Guards regiments in St Petersburg tolerating their new Tsar's Prussophile sentiments. Within a few days of concluding his alliance with Frederick, Peter III was forced by a palace revolution to abdicate in favour of his wife, Catherine II, and within another week he died a mysterious death. Catherine refused to become Frederick's ally, but at least she also refused to take any further part in the war. The coalition against Frederick was broken.

The Swedes, who had participated only half-heartedly in the long campaigns, used the opportunity of Russia's defection to withdraw entirely from the war in May 1762. Technically, fighting continued for another nine months, with the Prussians re-capturing the fortress of Schweidnitz from the Austrians and successfully resisting Daun's probes along the border between Saxony and

166

Constantinople

Silesia. But by the winter of 1762–3 the diplomats were busier than the soldiers. Peace preliminaries through Sardinian intermediaries in the British and French capitals led to the definitive Treaty of Paris of 10 February 1763, which ended the Anglo–French colonial war. Five days later, the representatives of Austria, Saxony and Prussia signed the Treaty of Hubertusburg, by which peace was restored in central Europe, with each state retaining the frontiers of 1756. Frederick promised to vote for Maria Theresa's eldest

Rufsie

ABOVE LEFT A satirical print
of Catherine II of Russia,
who forced her husband
Peter III to abdicate in her
favour. One week later he
mysteriously died. Although
she refused to become
Frederick's ally, at least she
kept her troops away from
his lands.

ABOVE Medallions struck to
celebrate the Treaty of
Hubertusburg, showing the
faces of Peter III of Russia
and Frederick.

169

surviving son, the Archduke Joseph, at the next Imperial Election; Maria Theresa dropped the style 'Duchess of Upper and Lower Silesia' from her title, a final renunciation of the lost province; and the two sovereigns pledged themselves to lasting friendship. The last of the troops were to be withdrawn from occupied Prussia and from Saxony by the end of March. It was, as observers had long anticipated, a peace of exhaustion rather than of triumph, but at least Frederick preserved his territories intact. At the cost of half a million of his subjects' lives – one-ninth of the total population of the kingdom – Frederick confirmed Prussia's status as a European power. In a war of survival, he survived, and the new kingdom he was painfully creating survived with him, though at a terrible cost.

An apt allegory of the Seven
Years' War showing a game
of billiards in progress over
the map of Europe.

7 The Patriarch King

FREDERICK CELEBRATED HIS FIFTY-FIRST BIRTHDAY during the last weeks of the Seven Years' War. He was now grey-haired, a wizened figure on horseback already bent with rheumatism and arthritis, a prematurely old man, sad in spirit and racked with pain. Only his eyes remained alert and observant, and there was much they would rather not have seen. He spent the closing stages of the long campaign at Leipzig. The problems of reconstruction were formidable and he was in no hurry to return to Berlin and face the realities of administration. His mood was sombre. When Prince Henry congratulated him on the Peace of Hubertusburg, he replied gravely, 'Had the State acquired some new province or other, it would have gratified me, but since that depended not on me but on Fortune, the thought does not make my mind restless. If I repair adequately the ravages of war, I shall have achieved something worth while, and that is now the limit of my ambitions'. He revisited the battlefield of Torgau and, during his final journey back to Berlin, he insisted on making a detour to Kunersdorf where he noted, with dismay, the devastation in the countryside on both sides of the Oder. There were too many ghosts in his mind for him to enjoy celebrating peace.

When he arrived at the gates of Berlin on the evening of 30 March he found that the city authorities expected him to ride through the streets in a special gilded coach, a Roman triumph by torchlight. But he was far too moved by the occasion to gratify the Berliners that night. He slipped as unobtrusively as possible into the palace by a side gate, postponing the ceremonial drive until he had conquered his emotions. Inside the palace he met for the first time in several years his Queen and her brother, Ferdinand of Brunswick. Frederick knew how to thank Ferdinand for his services to the State, but his tongue failed him when he was faced by the wife he respected but could not love. 'Madame has grown fatter', he said by way of greeting. It was an odd homecoming.

He wasted little time on the festivities of peace. When a delegation of local commissioners waited on him with a loyal address the morning after his return to the city, he cut short their elaborate compliments: 'Have you something to write with?' he asked. 'Very well. Now note this down. You gentlemen must draw up a list showing how much rye is needed for bread, how much seed, and how many horses and oxen and cows are needed at once in your districts. Think it over carefully and report back to me on the day after tomorrow'. The King was determined to give the wounds of war every opportunity to heal speedily.

PREVIOUS PAGES The Neues Palais at Potsdam c. 1770.

It is difficult to assess the amount of devastation in the kingdom. Frederick himself declared the invading armies had left the countryside in such a sorry state that he was reminded of the effects of the Thirty Years' War, which crippled parts of Germany for two or three generations. But it is possible he exaggerated. Some areas escaped comparatively lightly: Königsberg, for example, though occupied by the Russians, had been treated generously in return for acknowledging Empress Elizabeth's suzerainty over the city. This particular affront so riled Frederick that he refused to visit Königsberg for the rest of his reign and imposed heavy taxes on the old coronation city for the benefit of less fortunate parts of the kingdom, but at least Königsberg could afford them. Silesia had suffered greatly, as much from the Prussian army as from the invaders. Elsewhere there were, to a surprising degree, marked differences between neighbouring districts, the variations depending upon the actual route taken by troops on the march. As a preliminary move, Frederick ordered army horses to be made available to the farmers, and military stores distributed where famine threatened that winter, and as a long-term measure he sent men whom he could personally trust into the former war zones with instructions to prepare for him a survey of what needed to be done.

By the late spring of 1763 Frederick thus had a remarkable collection of statistics to hand. In Pomerania he found the problem of rehabilitation was relatively straightforward: 1,246 peasant homes had been destroyed; the peasants were given fifty thalers each and enough wood to rebuild their cottages. But in Silesia the official return listed 6,140 homes destroyed, together with more than 2,500 barns and nearly 5,000 stables. The King liked the people of Silesia (whom he insisted were more industrious than the Brandenburgers) and he gave special attention to their problems, spending some weeks each year in residence at Breslau. The textile industry in Silesia had somehow survived the war and enabled the province to pay its quota of taxes regularly, and Frederick was fully aware of the region's potential. The needs of the province, both in the towns and the countryside, had high priority. It says much for Frederick's forcefulness that when he made a tour of inspection through Silesia three years after the end of the war, he found that 5,496 houses had been rebuilt, together with nearly all the barns and four-fifths of the stables. From Breslau, on 1 September 1766, Frederick sent an enthusiastic letter to Voltaire:

A labourer seeking work
after the ravages of the
Seven Years' War.

Here I am in a province which prefers physical reality to metaphysics; they cultivate their fields, they have rebuilt eight thousand houses [sic!] and each year they give birth to thousands of children, replacing those who perished through the fury of politics and war . . . Landowners and people, busy with their tasks of recovery, live in peace, and they have so much work to do that nobody pays any attention to the beliefs of his neighbour. The embers of religious hatred, so often rekindled before the war, are extinct; and the spirit of tolerance grows daily in the people's habits of thought.

How fortunate for Silesia to have been annexed by Prussia and subjected to twelve years of war's fury!

There is no doubt that after the Peace of Hubertusburg, as after the Peace of Dresden, Frederick was convinced the Prussian monarchy desperately needed to free itself from the incubus of

176

war. 'I am returning to a city where endless tasks await me,' he wrote in March 1763, 'but where my bones must soon find a sanctuary never again disturbed by war, misfortune or human pettiness.' The kingdom could not stand the strain of further campaigns. Frederick wished to keep the army strong and efficient because he was still conscious his lands were territorially fragmented and an open invitation to an aggressive neighbour. But he was eager to complete the work of post-war reconstruction, if only to increase the revenue on which he could base the annual military budget. At heart he remained true to the theories of mercantilism and scientific agriculture he had championed in the decade of peace. He was willing for the State to supply livestock and seeds for the farmers of Brandenburg but he did not hide his conviction that there was a fundamental weakness in the agrarian economy of the whole region. More and more trees had to be planted in the sandy soil (which he once described as Germany's 'Libya'), and he commended landowners able to turn this scrub land into pasture. It pleased him especially to hear of cows grazing along the banks of the Oder, where a few years before he had sought death from a Russian bullet rather than accept defeat.

Frederick also resumed his policy of sponsored immigration. Before the Seven Years' War he had encouraged specifically skilled craftsmen to assist Prussia's young domestic industries, but for the last twenty years of his reign he invited any able-bodied man to settle with his family, either as an industrial worker or a peasant 'colonist'. Many of these 'new Prussians' continued to come from other parts of Germany, but Frederick was prepared to go farther afield, and he even established an immigration agency in Venice, the most cosmopolitan centre in southern Europe outside the Turkish Empire. At times Frederick used to maintain in conversation that the introduction of an entirely new racial stock in Prussia was desirable for the general well-being of the peasantry, and he amused himself by suggesting he might build a mosque in Berlin. But there would seem to be no reason for treating the hypotheses of his table-talk as earnestly as did the Prussian bureaucrats whom it alarmed.

The passage of years made Frederick care less and less about his popularity. He assumed he knew what was best for the peasantry and townsfolk just as he had always known precisely where to place his army during the wars. Obedience remained for him the prime civic virtue, and he expected an order to be carried out in civilian life as in a military camp. Often his words were misunder-

OPPOSITE A portrait of
Frederick. At this time he
was harnessing all the
energy he had shown
in warfare to the
reconstruction of the
Prussian State.

stood and his instructions bungled, but mistakes of this type never
surprised him: he had a profound contempt for the intelligence of
petty officials, and, for that matter, of most executive ministers
as well. Towards veterans of his wars he naturally felt a comradely
sympathy: during his tours of inspection he listened to their complaints, and often he personally received their petitions at Potsdam. The years of war not only aged him, they made a patriarchal
figure, 'Old Fritz', the stern head of a reluctant family. The
Junkers, the great landowners who bred the Prussian officer corps,
had been especially hard hit by the war, which ravaged their
Brandenburg estates: the King helped restore their fortunes by
favourable mortgage arrangements and even by direct donations
from his own limited funds. But his gratitude was tempered by a
realistic ruthlessness: bourgeois officers, hurriedly commissioned
during the last phase of the war, lost their new-found status with
the return of peace, and professional officers reverted to their
normal substantive rank, Prince Henry suddenly finding himself,
with some indignation, a mere colonel. On the other hand,
Frederick assumed that the sons of the nobility, having rendered
him loyal duty in the officer corps, had a natural right to hold posts
of administration in civil government. As a shrewd French observer noted in the closing years of the reign, in Prussia the State
was a servant of the army.

Frederick believed in enlightened administration to a greater
extent than the hidebound Tories who were his chief executants.
He continued to make detailed tours of inspection, attending to
localized problems as well as to matters of importance to the
kingdom as a whole. Distant municipal appointments, roads need-
ing repair, lagging projects of re-forestation, outmoded forms of
feudal serfdom, public buildings mouldering in decay – all these
matters, great and small, were observed, noted in writing, filed
away and used as a means of goading officials into action.
Frederick's visitations remained, as they had been before the war,
a series of earth tremors disturbing the routine of provincial life for
weeks after the first impact; but now what followed was, as often
as not, a new assessment of local taxation rather than a beneficial
reform, as in the earlier years of the reign. The King's views on
agriculture and the better use of land were almost always more
far-sighted than those of his administrators, but all too frequently
his good intentions were frustrated by the intractable nature of the
problems challenging him, by the procrastination of the Junker
landowners, and by his own tendency to become absorbed in

178

FRIDERICUS MAGNUS

fresh business before carrying through what had already been started.

In 1763, soon after the ending of the wars, the King rode into Pomerania and gave orders to the local Provincial Chamber for 'the suppression of all serfdom . . . immediately, completely and without question. Opposition will be countered by kindness, but if necessary by force, so that all will conform to the irrevocable decision of the King'. The nobility thereupon informed Frederick that he was mistaken: serfdom, though protected as a nobleman's right by seventeenth-century ordinances, had long since been transformed into a form of hereditary dependence, and the land-owners suggested that His Majesty might wish to safeguard the rights of the free peasantry by new legislation. Twelve months after his original order the King accordingly decreed that the peasants of Pomerania should be neither sold nor given away; they might sell anything they themselves owned, but they were ex-pected to pay their masters an annual rent, to render them labour service by themselves and their children, and they were forbidden to leave their homes without their masters' permission. Technic-ally, therefore, Frederick ensured that there was no serfdom in

180

Pomerania, but the precise relationship between landowner and peasant rested upon monetary tribute and compulsory duties. Although the condition of the peasantry varied from province to province, there was some truth in Frederick's own admission that the peasant was 'human society's universal beast of burden'. The best he could do for them was to punish excessive cruelty by a landowner or royal bailiff when it came to his notice and to forbid the enclosure of peasant holdings.

For all his alleged sympathy with the Enlightenment, Frederick never questioned the basic structure of society in the kingdom. The nobility had, he thought, natural virtues of command and, despite the narrowness of its outlook, deserved to have its privileges protected; only in East Prussia and in Silesia were the nobles required to pay any of the land tax, which the King levied uniformly on the peasants. The burghers served the State by commerce and industry: they were not allowed to acquire the status of landowners, and they were normally exempt from military duties; they contributed to the national income by heavy indirect taxation. The function of the peasant was equally clear in Frederick's mind: he rendered service to his master, he supplied recruits for the

The *Régie*, the hated body of French tax-collectors imported by Frederick to administer the economy, on its way to Berlin to take up its duties.

181

army, and he paid taxes, with probably as much as two-fifths of his earnings going to the State.

Fortunately for Frederick, the Prussians were a docile people and there was never any danger of revolt during his reign. The burden of taxation was, in general, lighter on the mass of the people than in Maria Theresa's Austrian lands or in Louis xv's France. Yet Frederick's ministers were aware of the danger of imposing more taxes, and on this count they took issue with the King in 1766. Frederick gave scant attention to their complaints. He established a new department of state, the so-called *Régie*, a body controlled by French experts in taxation, who were paid more than four times as much as the Prussian civil servants and permitted a bonus on every increase in excise duties which they were able to collect. With a royal monopoly on the sale of salt and tobacco (and, for the last five years of the reign, on coffee too), Frederick's financial policy came to arouse more resentment than any other measures of his reign. The fact that he felt compelled to farm out the *Régie* to imported Frenchmen was interpreted both by the taxpayers and the Prussian civil servants as a national insult.

Most of the increased revenue was absorbed by the needs of the army, which within a few years of the Peace of Hubertusburg again attained the level of 150,000 men. Remarkably little money was spent by Frederick on his own personal pleasures. The only personal extravagance of the second half of his reign was the building of the Neues Palais at Potsdam, slightly over a mile to the west of Sans Souci. The new palace cost the King about half a million pounds to build and furnish. Work began on the foundations in the summer of 1763 and it was completed six years later. The architect, Johann Büring, had none of Knobelsdorff's lightness of touch, nor did Frederick himself take any great interest in Büring's work. The grandiose façades, heavily colonnaded, convey a sense of power; with its hundred-feet-long marble concert hall and its theatre for five hundred, it is more a parade palace than a royal residence. The King visited it only on formal occasions, preferring to live in Sans Souci. Probably the principal reason for building the palace was to provide employment for the craftsmen of Berlin, though it had a symbolic value as an assurance that the wars were really at an end.

Frederick's personal tastes changed little. He dutifully entertained his nephews and nieces from time to time, but he showed far more affection towards his whippets and greyhounds. His interest in the French Enlightenment was unabated: he continued

182

to exchange letters with Voltaire once or twice a month; he read Rousseau's *Emile* soon after the return of peace, and thought little of it or its author, and for nine weeks in the summer of 1763 he entertained the great mathematician and philosopher d'Alembert, whom he found such agreeable company that he maintained correspondence with him for another twenty years. Rather unexpectedly, Frederick established a literary friendship with the Bavarian-born Electress of Saxony, Maria Antonia, whom he twice invited to week-long visits to Potsdam. Maria Antonia, the most cultivated princess in Germany, shared his love of music and literature: she composed an opera and, as she admitted in one of her letters, she delighted in drawing out his observations on philosophical problems. Their correspondence was conducted in a stilted artificial style, with shrewd judgements sometimes hidden by elaborate flattery, but it is clear that Frederick, misogynist though he remained at heart, respected Maria Antonia's character and intelligence. If, however, she hoped to influence his policy towards Saxony and Poland by her friendship, she was disappointed. Frederick always distinguished in his mind between his leisure pursuits and the business of government, and he did not welcome the intrusion of one in the other.

As he grew older, Frederick was forced more and more to attend to the detailed conduct of diplomacy. He had always made a point of personally reading and annotating the despatches of his envoys abroad, but for the first half of the reign, he did at least seek the advice of others before formulating his policy. He respected the views of Podewils, a trained diplomat, even though he generally thought him over-cautious. Podewils, however, died in 1760 and the King's later advisers on foreign affairs, Finckenstein and Hertzberg, lacked the old minister's personality or experience. Indeed, in the second half of the reign, the only man able to influence the King's foreign policy was his brother Henry, who visited St Petersburg in the winter of 1770-1 and worked skilfully for a Russo–Prussian understanding on the Polish question. There was, however, another reason for the King's increased diplomatic activity. After 1763 the pattern of international relations on the European continent underwent a remarkable change: France, anxious for a war of revenge against Britain for her colonial losses, withdrew from active involvement in German affairs, content with the balance of interests between Habsburgs and Hohenzollerns and, at the same time, Austrian policy recovered the initiative, largely through the influence of the Archduke Joseph, Maria

The Emperor Joseph II of
Austria, eldest son of Maria
Theresa, and in Frederick's
opinion, the most dangerous
and ambitious Habsburg for
two hundred years.

Theresa's eldest son (who succeeded his father Francis as Emperor
in 1765). It was essential for Frederick personally to use his prestige
and reputation within Germany to counter Joseph's designs. He
was convinced Joseph was the most ambitious and militaristic
Habsburg for two centuries, and he warned his nephew and heir,
Frederick William, that Joseph ultimately sought not merely the
recovery of Silesia, but the total elimination of the Prussian

184

Maria Antonia, the Electress
of Saxony, with whom
Frederick corresponded
avidly about literature
and music.

monarchy. For the moment, Frederick was prepared to collaborate
with Joseph, provided the young Emperor respected Prussia's
status, but he did not trust him.

Frederick's surest guarantee against a revival of Austrian power
was his understanding with Catherine II of Russia. Although
Catherine did not share her murdered husband's admiration for
everything Prussian, she was realistic enough to see collaboration

185

RIGHT A portrait of Frederick in old age.

LEFT and BELOW Officers and hussars
from the Hussar regiment.

FRIDERICUS II. REX.

with Frederick would allow her to strengthen Russia's hold on Poland. Frederick had always wanted to absorb the corridor of Polish territory which separated East Prussia from Brandenburg, and Catherine at her accession made it clear to her ministers that she favoured the eventual acquisition of Poland's most eastern lands so as to advance the Russian frontier to the River Dvina and provide direct contact between the Russian-held port of Riga and the citizens of Smolensk and Moscow. But neither Russia nor Prussia was prepared to annex Polish territories outright without careful diplomatic preparation, partly because of mutual distrust and partly from fear that such a drastic solution would lead to another general war in Europe. Hence, in April 1764, the Prussians and Russians signed a defensive alliance valid for eight years (and renewed for a further eight) and undertook to place a Polish noble-man, Stanislas Poniatowski, on the throne in Warsaw in succession to Augustus III, who had died the previous autumn. They also agreed to maintain the existing Polish constitution, and Catherine kept an army of fifty thousand men on the middle Vistula so as to assist Poniatowski to follow a policy which was acceptable to his powerful protectors.

These proposals were not an ideal solution of the Polish question, as Frederick knew well enough. Catherine insisted on protecting the rights of the Orthodox and Protestant minorities against the Polish Roman Catholic nobility, an exercise of Russian interference in Polish affairs much resented by the great Polish families. By the summer of 1768 the Russians were faced by a guerrilla resistance movement in eastern Poland, and there was a danger that patriotic associations would menace the communications between Brandenburg and East Prussia. The following year Frederick suggested to the Russians that the time had come for Poland's three neighbours (Russia, Prussia and Austria) to agree on the acquisition of the vital border regions so as to safeguard their own interests without conflict. But Catherine, already engaged in a major war with the Turks, showed little interest in Frederick's project. 'There is in Poland', she wrote, 'a fortunate anarchy which we can manipulate at our will.'

Frederick disliked shaping his policy to Russian needs. He was afraid the successes of Catherine's armies against the Turks would so disturb the balance of power in south-eastern Europe that the Austrians would be forced to intervene. This would pose for him an awkward dilemma: should he remain true to his Russian alliance and fight a war he could not afford, or should he break with

OPPOSITE An allegory entitled 'The Kings' Cake', showing Frederick, Stanislaus Poniatowski, Joseph II and Catherine II carving up Poland.

OPPOSITE Frederick and
Joseph II embracing at
Neustadt in Moravia.
Although Joseph's mother,
Maria Theresa, was deeply
mistrustful of Frederick, the
uneasy friendship continued
for as long as they shared
the common pursuit of
sharing out Poland.

Russia and accept total diplomatic isolation? To his relief, he was saved from this embarrassment by an Austrian proposal that Vienna and Berlin should work together in order to keep Germany neutral. 'There is nothing we can do more sensible', Frederick replied, 'We are Germans, and what does it matter to us if . . . the Turks and Russians are busy pulling each other apart by the hair? The Queen-Empress and I have long fought out ruinous wars, but what have they left to separate us?' In the last week of August 1769 Frederick welcomed the Emperor Joseph to the fortress of Neisse in Silesia and for four days entertained him in a city which had been a Habsburg possession until 1742. Frederick exerted himself to charm the twenty-eight-year-old Emperor, who duly informed his mother of the King's generous sentiments. Maria Theresa, who had a long and bitter memory, was not convinced of her old enemy's sincerity, but there was an outward reconciliation between the two leading German dynasties, and Catherine of Russia was impressed by the demonstration.

A year later Frederick repaid Joseph's visit, crossing to Neustadt in Moravia. Joseph brought with him from Vienna the great Noverre (who mounted a ballet for the King's entertainment) and also Prince Kaunitz, who talked at length to Frederick over Polish affairs. Less than eight weeks after the meeting, Maria Theresa's troops seized the small duchy of Zips, in the Carpathian mountains. The duchy had been a Polish possession for over three hundred years, but in Vienna Kaunitz maintained that Zips was historically part of the Hungarian kingdom. Frederick was delighted at the Austrian move. 'Now,' he told his envoy to St Petersburg, 'there can no longer be any question of preserving Poland intact.' If the Austrians took Zips, he would have all the lower Vistulan lands, including the port of Danzig.

There were still hurdles to overcome. The least serious of them was the Polish Diet, whose members could be bought or bullied into acquiescence. Catherine disliked giving Prussia control of the lower Vistula, but was willing to accept a compromise which denied Prussia the cities of Danzig and Thorn (Gdansk and Torun). The chief opposition came from Maria Theresa who, on reflection, strongly disapproved of Joseph's initiative in seizing Zips and claimed that any further acquisition of Polish territory was political brigandage, inimical to her standards of diplomatic behaviour. But by the end of the year Joseph had convinced his mother that if Russia and Prussia acquired Polish territory with the consent of the Polish Diet, then it was essential for Austria to associate herself

OVERLEAF A map showing
the partitions of Poland.
Although, on paper,
Frederick received the
smallest portion, the gain
of 'West Prussia' fulfilled
one of his lifelong political
ambitions.

190

with the act of partition in order to preserve the European equilibrium. The treaties of partition were drawn up in St Petersburg in January and February 1772 and finally signed ('in the name of the Most Sacred Trinity') in the following August, although it was not until the spring of 1773 that the Polish Diet ratified the settlement.

The Partition of 1772 ceded rather more than a quarter of the Polish lands. Russia absorbed half of the ceded territories, with a population of some two million; Austria took a third, with a population of two and a half million; and Prussia received the remaining one-sixth, with six hundred thousand inhabitants. On paper, therefore, Frederick had the worst of the bargain. Strategically, however, 'West Prussia' had an importance far greater than its size. At last the King had achieved one of his principal objectives, the incorporation of all north-eastern Germany under the Prussian Crown.

In the summer of 1772, shortly before the final convention was concluded, Frederick travelled to the Vistula and inspected the lands promised to him. He was well pleased with what they promised. To his brother Henry, he wrote:

It is an excellent and highly advantageous gain for us, politically and financially, but, to arouse less jealousy, I am saying to anyone who wants to hear my views that throughout my journey I have seen only sand, conifers, heather and Jews. Certainly it will mean much work . . . for there is no system or order here, and the towns are in a deplorable state . . . Yet commercially we have the best of the bargain. We shall be masters of everything Poland produces or imports, which is considerable. Best of all, our control over the wheat trade will always save us from famine.

In March 1775 a commercial treaty was negotiated with the authorities in Warsaw which provided Frederick's excise-men with the right to levy a twelve per cent value tax on Polish river traffic along the Vistula to Danzig, a toll which brought a steady revenue to the Prussian treasury and helped to keep down the price of Prussian grain in competition with Polish grain in the Baltic trade. Frederick was as ruthless a mercantilist as he was a soldier.

For the remaining decade of his reign West Prussia and its problems occupied more of the King's working hours than any other of his provinces. As earlier with Silesia, Frederick retained direct administration of the new lands in his own hands, systematically encouraging the establishment of German 'colonies' of artisans or peasants, setting up new villages, assessing schemes for draining marshes and damming rivers, approving plans for a canal

193

from the Oder to the Vistula and for developing the small port of Elbing as a rival to Danzig, and introducing into this 'barbarous region' the fiscal and legal systems already functioning in Brandenburg and East Prussia. Despite Frederick's claim to have had the best of the bargain, West Prussia was more backward in 1772 than the Austrian acquisition, Galicia. Although, as Frederick himself admitted, the Prussians had no legal title to the Polish lands, at least he saw to it that the people of West Prussia enjoyed a higher standard of life than did their compatriots in rump Poland or in the regions ceded to Russia and Austria.

Gratitude for material advantages did not, of course, reconcile the younger generation of Poles to the enlightened rule of an alien

patriarch. Even if Frederick was unaware of the power of patriotic sentiment, he was uneasy in his conscience over the partitions. To d'Alembert he explained that the province had been allowed to sink into decay through the incompetence of the Polish administration, 'the worst government in Europe apart from that of the Turks'. He struck a similar note of moral rectitude in his correspondence with Voltaire: 'It is unreasonable', he wrote proudly in December 1773, 'that the country which gave birth to Copernicus should be left to moulder in the barbarism that results from tyranny'. It is true that West Prussia already contained a solid basis of German Protestant families, who were far easier to assimilate in a Prussian state than were the predominantly Polish

Prussia saw the rise of a new trading class under the rule of Frederick, and enormous energy was diverted into the digging of canals and the improvement of communications: a contemporary illustration of a trade convoy being hauled through a canal.

or Ruthene peoples of Galicia in the Habsburg Empire. But Frederick had given Prussia her first non-German minority; by so doing he began a process which led to the partitions of 1793 and 1795 and the complete destruction of the Polish state. Almost certainly he never wished Poland swept from the map, if only because he did not want his successors burdened with the responsibility of preserving the borderlands of Europe from Russian greed – that, he thought, was a better historic mission for Catholic Poland and Catholic Austria than for his own sprawling kingdom. He failed to realize that, by assisting two other great powers to hasten the demise of the sick man of central Europe, he was defying the logic of historical tradition for mere political convenience. Maria Theresa's instinct was right: the partition of Poland created a dangerously revolutionary precedent, from which, in the Napoleonic era, all Germany was to suffer.

OPPOSITE D'Alembert, the brilliant French mathematician and philosopher, who was a great admirer of Frederick. Despite this, he resisted all Frederick's efforts to persuade him to settle in Berlin as head of the Academy.

8
Patron
Saint

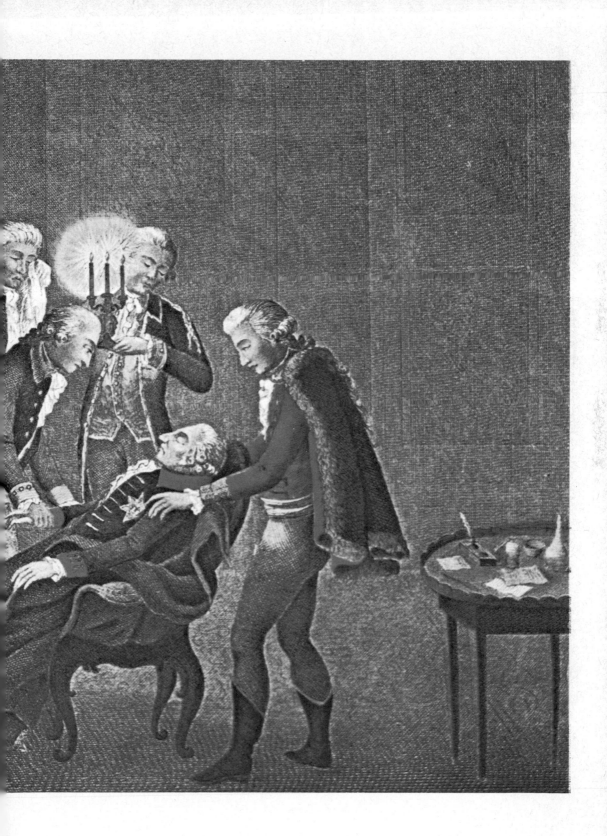

THE POLISH PARTITIONS HAD ONE INDIRECT CONSEQUENCE.
Frederick secured recognition from the Emperor Joseph and
from Catherine II of his right to be styled 'King *of* Prussia'. It was a
title which had been current in Berlin ever since his accession, but
technically he had remained merely 'King *in* Prussia', as his father
and grandfather before him. Joseph's acceptance of the changed
style was significant, for it appeared to raise the status of Prussian
kingship in relation to the Imperial primacy within Germany. It
remained to be seen whether the Emperor had raised no objections
because he did not wish to dispute the niceties of constitutional
semantics, or whether he was prepared to accept the newly found
power of Prussia as a basis for sharing the political control of
Germany. Joseph's arrogant character and evident desire to
strengthen the hold of the Habsburgs on southern Germany made
it unlikely he would favour 'Dualism' in the old Reich. Frederick
had few illusions about the man who had entertained him at
Neustadt, and Joseph had long since overcome his youthful enthusiasm for the enlightened autocrat of Berlin.

During the negotiations over Poland, Frederick had been
obliged to work closely with both the Russians and the Austrians.
The experience had not lessened his suspicion of Joseph and
Kaunitz, nor had it inclined him to put much faith in Catherine's
good intentions. He believed – and with reason – that the Russians
resented Prussia's stranglehold on Vistulan trade and that Joseph
was ready to exploit any crisis in German affairs so as to find
territorial compensation for the loss of Silesia. In the closing
months of 1775, while Frederick was confined to his room with
chronic gout, his agents reported that Joseph was concentrating a
large army along Austria's north-western borders. The news was a
tonic for the King. He was certain Joseph intended to march if
Prussia were thrown into confusion by his protracted illness or
death. His strength rallied and there was no more talk of troops on
the move in Bohemia; but Frederick remained convinced he would
have to risk another war with 'Dame Theresa and Joseph Caesar',
or acquiesce in a restoration of Habsburg primacy throughout
Germany.

On the last day of the year 1777 the Elector of Bavaria died,
childless. The succession was in doubt; Joseph himself agreed to
back one branch of the Wittelsbach dynasty only on condition that
Lower Bavaria was ceded to Austria; Frederick, predictably, supported the claims of the other main contender for the succession. 'I
know that these princes of the Empire are a collection of wretched

PREVIOUS PAGES The death
of Frederick, painted by
P. Haas.

200

nonentities', Frederick wrote to his brother, Henry, early in March 1778, 'and I have no intention of becoming their Don Quixote; but if we let Austria exercise despotic power within Germany we provide her with arms for use against ourselves . . . I regard war as unavoidable: the Emperor wants it and his armies are massing'. None of Frederick's senior commanders believed the situation was as serious as the King maintained, and Henry pointedly intimated he thought his brother was shadow-acting past triumphs. But on 6 April 1778 Frederick set out for field headquarters in Silesia, and three months later pitted his army once more against the Sudeten mountains, hoping to seize Olmütz and march on Vienna.

The 'War of the Bavarian Succession', a grandiose title for an insignificant episode, lasted for nine months. It did not enhance Frederick's military reputation: he won no victories and suffered no defeats, for in the whole campaign he could not once bring Laudon and Lacy to battle. They remained entrenched in fortified camps and watched the rain fall (which it did that late summer and autumn with unusual persistence). When Frederick sought to outmanoeuvre the enemy, he was checked by the impassable roads and the constant torrent of water down the mountain paths. It was no longer possible for him to feed his troops regularly or get hay for the horses. Morale was low and there were mass desertions. At first Frederick tried to stir up enthusiasm for the war, steeling his tortured body to remain for ten hours in the saddle so as to set

Prussian troops in 1803. Seventeen years after Frederick's death they still wear the same uniforms.

Frederick's memorial in
Potsdam, in front of the
Garrison Church where he is
buried.

an example to his officers and men. But when the rain gave way to
mist and fog, he abandoned any hope of bringing the campaign
to the boil. Discipline was kept by a more savage system of punish-
ment than in earlier wars. Frederick seemed uninterested in his
men and it was only in March, when peace talks began at Teschen
under French mediation, that he showed any spirit. The succession

202

question in Bavaria was settled by a compromise which recognized all legitimate claims; Joseph received a mere thirty-six square miles of Bavarian territory; and Frederick was assured that the Hohenzollerns would eventually inherit the small Margravates of Ansbach and Bayreuth. Everyone's face was saved and the King hurried back to Potsdam, where the royal company of actors

mounted a season of Racine tragedies to purge his pent-up emotions.

Prince Henry criticized his brother's decision to go to war and his handling of the army. Patiently Frederick explained that he had gained what he wanted from the campaign: recognition, among the German princes, of Prussia's right to defend the existing order against Imperial pretensions. But Henry was not convinced. He retired to Rheinsberg (which Frederick had handed over to him when Sans Souci was completed) and there he attracted all the disappointed officers and nobility who cavilled at the King's conduct of affairs. In Russia or France the establishment of such an opposition court would have alarmed the sovereign and, at best, caused him to modify his policy. But Frederick, though sardonically amused to find his beloved Rheinsberg becoming a haven for the disaffected, ignored their grumbles and complaints, knowing that the strict code of the officer corps guaranteed loyalty and obedience. He continued to champion 'Germany' against the Empire, especially after Maria Theresa's death in 1780, when there was no longer any restraint at the Viennese Court on Joseph's ambitions. The last initiative of Frederick in foreign affairs was to found a League of Princes in 1785. Its members, who included Roman Catholic as well as Protestant rulers, pledged themselves to preserve their rights and possessions in the German lands against the claims of the Emperor. Old age had made the rebel King of the 1740s a pillar of German conservatism, seeking refuge from a reforming Emperor in custom and tradition. Frederick had never been so popular among his brother sovereigns of the German states as in those closing months of his reign.

His own subjects respected him and feared him, but they did not love him. Goethe, visiting Berlin in 1778, was shocked at the ingratitude of the people towards the sovereign who had made the city a genuine capital. They resented his continued exclusion of the bourgeoisie from titles of nobility, or more precisely from owning landed estates, and no one in the urban middle-class or the town labourers, had forgiven the King his introduction of snooping French excise-men. Yet they knew he was no extravagant libertine, wasting his hours on frivolities. They accepted the tale (which was indeed true) that he still rose each morning at four and continued to work through the details of administration until he had cleared his desk of accumulated papers. His subjects were prepared to stand bareheaded in the street as his carriage went by, often mustering a cheer for the bowed figure, 'badly dressed and covered with dust'. They were amused by his eccentricities: by the free-

OPPOSITE At the end of his reign, Frederick was a pillar of conservatism, a rock in a rapidly changing continent. This allegory, executed a year before his death, shows him (*right*) with the princes of Hanover and Saxony, forming a bond.

dom he allowed his dogs, as they ravaged the curtains of the palace corridors or followed their master, never quite to heel; by stories of his eating habits, the old King complaining of stomach pains and yet consuming heavily spiced dishes washed down with cold coffee into which he had poured champagne; and by his use of a camel (said to have come from southern Russia) which, before the King went into residence in the capital for Christmas, conveyed a load of books and snuffboxes along the seventeen-mile route from Potsdam, an annual event which prompted heavy jokes about the increasingly sandy nature of Brandenburg soil. The English diplomat James Harris noticed ten years before Frederick's death the 'motley composition of barbarity and humanity which so strongly mark his character' and shrewdly commented on the ease with which his 'humane, benevolent and friendly' qualities forsook him 'the instant he acts in his royal capacity'. The dissimulation forced upon him in youth scarred his character to the very end. To young officers meeting him for the first time at manœuvres or in the banquets he gave at the Neues Palais after the Potsdam reviews, their King seemed a sad and terrifying old man, soured by his knowledge of others and of himself.

Most of the guest rooms at Sans Souci were closed and shuttered in the last six or seven years of his reign, and there were only occasional echoes of past brilliance around the table. The King still sharpened his tired wits in the company of a few intimates. His last chamberlain was the young Italian, the Marquese Lucchesini, with whom he enjoyed talking of the arts and particularly of the Italian cities, which it grieved him he had never visited. Occasionally, for the benefit of foreign visitors, Frederick would exert himself and play his favourite role, the supreme Philosopher-King of the Age of Reason. The Prince de Ligne (who was himself to carry the grace and wit of eighteenth-century society through the Napoleonic period to the Congress of Vienna) visited Frederick at Potsdam in 1779, and found him still able to charm his guests with old-fashioned courtesies and captivate them by the range and elegance of his conversation. Ligne was surprised at the liveliness and animation in Frederick's features when he became interested in a topic of discussion. 'He talked', the Prince wrote later 'about every subject one can imagine, speaking without raising his voice, in a tone as pleasing as the movement of his lips, which was inexpressibly graceful.'

Yet there were limits to the King's intellectual comprehension, some of which left him out of touch with his subjects. Although

A portrait of Frederick and his wife in old age.

many of them were by now reading Lessing, Herder, Goethe and Schiller, Frederick continued to ignore the existence of German authors. He complained it was impossible for the Germans to have a vernacular literature until princely patrons encouraged their scholars to perfect and refine the language: 'Let us have some Medicis', he wrote in 1780, 'and we shall have some geniuses'. Nor was Frederick's myopic judgement confined exclusively to creative prose and verse. At Königsberg during these years one of Frederick's own subjects, the son of a saddler, was winning distinction for his lectures analysing 'Pure Reason'. Even senior Prussian civil servants, members of the aristocracy, listened to Professor Emmanuel Kant; but, since he lectured in a city Frederick would not visit and wrote in a language he would not read, there was never any prospect that he would stimulate a response from the

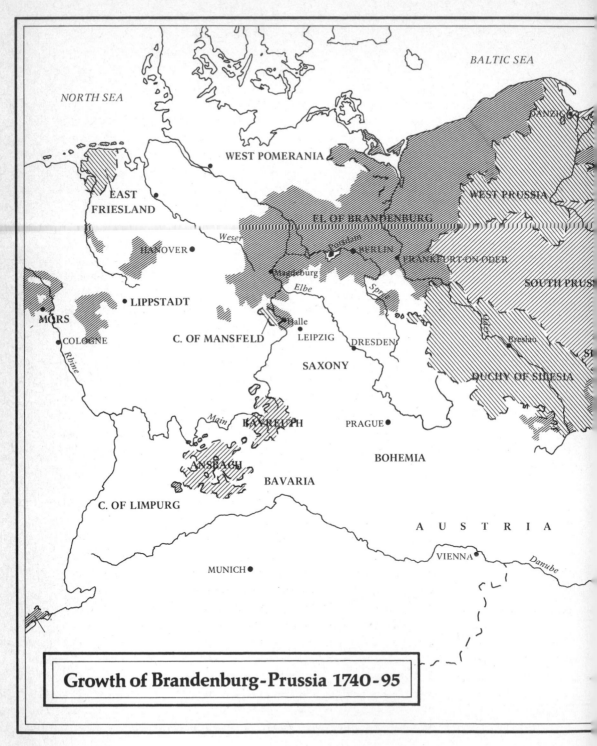

NORTH SEA

BALTIC SEA

WEST POMERANIA

EAST
FRIESLAND

DANZIG

WEST PRUSSIA

HANOVER

Weser

EL. OF BRANDENBURG

Potsdam

BERLIN

FRANKFURT-ON-ODER

SOUTH PRUSS

MORS

LIPPSTADT

Magdeburg

Elbe

Spr

Oder

Breslau

SI

COLOGNE

C. OF MANSFELD

Halle

LEIPZIG

DRESDEN

DUCHY OF SILESIA

Rhine

SAXONY

Main

BAYREUTH

PRAGUE

ANSBACH

BAVARIA

BOHEMIA

C. OF LIMPURG

A U S T R I A

MUNICH

VIENNA

Danube

Growth of Brandenburg-Prussia 1740-95

philosopher of Potsdam. Moreover, the King had read far too much Voltaire to appreciate metaphysics any longer, and Kant possessed pacifist sympathies inimical to his intellectual tolerance.

In the last week of August 1785 Frederick insisted on inspecting a regiment for several hours in heavy rain without a protective mantle. He became feverish, and never again fully recovered. His heir, Augustus William's eldest son, seemed to him so unintelligent and self-centred that there was no point in explaining policy to him. He had written him a political testament seventeen years before, and he declined to revise it, preferring to complete as many tasks as possible before his health finally failed. Most of the winter he spent at Potsdam, hoping the summer warmth would enable him to shake off asthma, from which he had now begun to suffer. It made little difference.

Despite his weakness, Frederick remained mentally curious. A Hanoverian doctor, summoned to him in the last weeks of June 1786, found the King very weak – but still wishing to cross-question him about Edward Gibbon's writings: the first three volumes of the *Roman Empire* had appeared but Frederick, to his irritation, had not been able to read them. Illness certainly did not mellow his character. Soon after the Hanoverian doctor's visit, Queen Elizabeth-Christine sent a letter asking if she might come to the sick-room. The reply was as coldly formal as ever: 'I am greatly obliged for the wishes you so kindly express, Madame, but a high fever which I have contracted prevents me from answering you'. It was the last communication between husband and wife.

Throughout the first fortnight of August the King continued to work as usual, examining plans for manœuvres in Silesia and the project for land reclamation in West Prussia over the following eighteen months. Penetrating questions showed his mind was still active. Did the military timetable make sufficient allowance for rain? Would the bread-waggons be able to get through to the regiments on the march? What precautions were being taken to prevent the Oder from flooding the new pasture land? Had the three hundred Spanish sheep his agents were purchasing in Castile for the royal domains yet arrived? Characteristically, he divided his attention between the state of the army and the state of agriculture. And it was equally characteristic he should have assumed that no one but the King could handle such details. Even on his deathbed he remained the first servant of the State, and its master.

But daily he was becoming weaker. On Tuesday, 15 August, he woke at five in the morning and approved some papers his council-

Testament

VOM 8·JANUAR

1769

Unser Leben führt uns mit raschen Schritten von der Geburt bis zum Tode. In dieser kurzen Zeit, spanne ist es die Bestimmung des Menschen, für das Wohl der Gemeinschaft, deren Mitglied er ist, zu arbeiten.

Seit dem Tage, da mir die Leitung der Geschäfte zufiel, war es mein ernstes Bemühen, mit allen Kräften, die mir die Natur verliehen, und nach Maßgabe meiner schwachen Einsicht den Staat den zu regieren ich die Ehre hatte, glücklich und blühend zu machen. Ich habe dem Recht und den Gesetzen zur Herrschaft verholfen, habe Ordnung und Klarheit in die Finanzen gebracht und im Heere die Mannszucht erhalten, die ihm seine Überlegenheit über die anderen Truppen Europas verschaffte.

Bis zum letzten Atemzuge werden meine Wünsche dem Glücke des Staates gelten. Möchte er stets mit Gerechtigkeit, Weisheit und Stärke regiert werden! Möchte er durch die Milde der Gesetze, der glücklichste, in seinen Finanzen der bestverwaltete und durch ein Heer, das nur nach Ehre und edlem Waffenruhm trachtet, der am tapfersten verteidigte sein! Möchte er blühen bis ans Ende der Zeiten! Friedrich.

lors brought him to study, although when they looked at them afterwards they saw his signature was scarcely legible. Next morning he did not wake until eleven o'clock, when he gave orders to the officer of the Guard and sank back in a stupor. In the evening he seemed to find new strength and made his reader select passages from Voltaire's *Louis XIV*, although he could not listen attentively. Suddenly he was seized by a fit of coughing and his aides thought he was dying, but still he held on to life. One of them leaned forward and heard him murmur, 'The mountain is behind us, we shall do better': was he thinking in metaphor of his kingdom, or was he haunted by some memory of campaigning along Austria's northern frontier with the plateaux of Moravia sloping down towards Vienna, the goal his armies never attained? Two hussars propped him up on a chair, helping him to breathe. At his feet a whippet bitch, sensing the tension of the hour, began to shiver with fright. The King noticed the dog's discomfort and told an orderly to find a blanket for the poor creature. It was his last command. At twotwenty in the morning of Thursday 17 August, Frederick died. By noon the Potsdam garrison had sworn an oath of allegiance to Frederick William II, the forty-two-year-old nephew whom the old King had so despised.

The French traveller Mirabeau – soon to win brief fame as a revolutionary statesman – described the mood of Berlin on hearing the news: 'Everything is dismal but nothing is sad', he wrote. 'There are no regrets, no sighs, no words of praise, nor is there here a face which does not show relief and hope.' No doubt the people of Berlin believed the burden of taxation would be eased with a less ambitious monarch on the throne, but Mirabeau cannot entirely be trusted as a chronicler. He had met Frederick only four months previously and the King, despite his normal partiality for the French aristocracy, had taken a dislike to him, which he did not trouble to disguise. Certainly a long procession of Berliners journeyed out to Potsdam to pay their respects to the hero-king's body as it lay in state at the old *Stadtschloss*. Frederick had asked to be buried on the terrace of Sans Souci, beside his favourite dogs and horse. But Frederick William II was too conventional to permit his uncle this one last gesture of contempt for mankind. Frederick was interred in a vault beneath the pulpit of the Garrison Church in Potsdam, beside the remains of his father. He was to be remembered, not as the crowned philosopher of an eccentric palace, but as the victor of Chotusitz, Hohenfriedberg, Rossbach and Leuthen. Dynastic sentiment was already beginning to weave a legend.

OPPOSITE Frederick's political testament, written seventeen years before his death. It is more a justification of his own behaviour than advice to his successor.

211

OPPOSITE Frederick's great-nephew, King Frederick William II, swearing eternal friendship with Alexander of Russia and his wife Queen Louise beside Frederick's tomb, 1805.

This legend, in the nineteenth century, inspired Prussia's kings, soldiers and statesmen to realize ambitions far beyond Frederick's most optimistic predictions. But for the first twenty years after his death there is no doubt that his influence condemned Prussian policy to ineffectual rigidity. Frederick William II did not possess his uncle's insight into world affairs nor his all-pervading sense of energy. Prussia experienced the disastrous consequences of government by a monarch who lacked the will to rule. Projects and enterprises begun under Frederick's patronage continued, largely of their own volition: thus the jurists Johann von Carmer and Karl Gottlieb, who had started to prepare a uniform legal code in the closing years of Frederick's reign, completed their task only in 1795, and engineers and navvies were still busy making the Oder navigable for sea-going vessels, digging new canals so that barges could convey goods from all over Prussia and Brandenburg to the Baltic. On the other hand, the new King did not understand the need for pliability in foreign affairs: he thought it logical to continue Frederick's policy blindly, persisting in the partitions of Poland even though Count Hertzberg, the veteran Foreign Minister, contended that his old master would have regarded the total disappearance of Poland as a victory for Russia. Frederick William II's obsession with his eastern frontier blinded him to the danger from revolutionary France. Although the Prussians participated in the campaigns of 1792-5, and won an early success at Longwy, the war was unpopular and the army thereafter was engaged in no battles of significance, nor was any attempt made to formulate a general strategy for containing the Revolution. The Prussians fought according to Frederick's strictures. For the most part, they were led by regimental commanders who learned all they knew of warfare as subalterns in Frederick's later campaigns. Against armies of the First French Republic, Frederick's training still held good, but already the idea of the nation in arms and the development of artillery was outdating the lessons of his twelve campaigns. The days of mercenaries and a slow baggage-train were finished.

In 1797 Frederick's great-nephew came to the throne, styling himself Frederick William III. As a lad of fifteen he had attended his great-uncle's last manœuvres. He was an amiable nonentity, proud of an army that thought itself invincible but a little afraid of his military heritage. Courage came to him from his Queen, the indomitable Louise of Mecklenburg-Strelitz, and from the flattery of Tsar Alexander I, favourite grandson of Catherine the Great

and himself an admirer of the Frederician military tradition. In the late autumn of 1805 Alexander came to Berlin, seeking to encourage the Prussians to join the Third Coalition against Napoleon. To symbolize the bonds of sympathy linking the Prussian and Russian autocracies, the King, the Tsar and Queen Louise went to the Garrison Church at Potsdam late at night on 4 November, and the two monarchs swore an oath of eternal

In 1806 the by then old-fashioned Frederician army crumpled before Napoleon. He too visited Frederick's tomb, reflecting that had Frederick been alive, he would not have reached Potsdam.

friendship over Frederick the Great's tomb. Tears of emotion ran down their cheeks as they bound their countries never to fight against each other. Politically and militarily the oath had little effect on policy. But it was a significant occasion: for the first time in her history Prussia possessed a national shrine – the burial place of her warrior King.

Almost exactly a year later the Frederician military system collapsed beneath the weight of Napoleon's twin victories at Jena and Auerstadt. Napoleon himself reached the outskirts of Berlin. Before entering the capital he insisted on descending with a group of senior commanders to the vault of the Garrison Church, to stand in silence beside Frederick's tomb. 'Off with your hats, gentlemen,' he said at last to his companions, 'Were he still alive, we should not now be here in Prussia.'

It was a sentiment shared by many Germans, but was it true? The army defeated by Napoleon was organized and trained by the methods perfected by Frederick more than forty years before Jena. In the closing years of his reign there had been critics of his military policy among the younger officers, but neither of Frederick's successors had welcomed original thought, least of all within the officer corps. The tragedy for Prussia – and for Frederick's reputation – is that the commanders of 1806 had been taught to assume that the rules of warfare were immutable, the essentials of strategy unchanging. Frederick himself triumphed in his earlier campaigns by discarding orthodox military precepts, but he imposed a new conformity on the army which made it ignore the innovations of the last decade of the century, spurning not only the ideas of the French but of Suvorov's Russians as well. Napoleon's remark was a tribute to the enduring power of Frederick's reputation, rather than a mature assessment. 'We slumbered on the laurels of Frederick the Great', Queen Louise admitted. What was needed in Prussia was the means to inject the old King's aggressive spirit into the mass army of the nineteenth century. It was found, ironically enough, by two non-Prussians: the Hanoverian-born General von Scharnhorst, who became Frederick William III's War Minister the year after Jena, and the Saxon General von Gneisenau, who assisted Scharnhorst to create the Prussian General Staff and a new officer corps, filled by men of 'knowledge, education . . . and outstanding bravery' rather than solely by the nobility.

After the campaign of 1813–14, when the Prussians marched with the Russians and Austrians westwards across the Rhine and

Of all the distorted views of Frederick, none has been so gross as those of the
Nazis. This film, made in 1941, begins at Frederick's lowest ebb, after the
disaster of the battle of Kunersdorf, and predictably traces his military
campaigns from strength to strength. In the final scene he enters Berlin to the
cheers of the massive crowd, and, according to the film handout: 'as the
conqueror of a world full of enemies. He has become the Great King!'

entered Paris, captured French flags were hung in the Garrison Church at Potsdam, as though to expiate Napoleon's visit. But the spirit that finally turned all Germany against the French Empire differed from any collective emotion of the Frederician era. Germany was liberated by a patriotic war for a common Fatherland. On the rare occasions when Frederick spoke of 'our Fatherland' – in the address to his commanders on the eve of Leuthen, for example, and in some of his later political writings – he was thinking purely in terms of his Brandenburg–Prussian heritage, an abstraction of which he believed only a few of the nobility were even conscious. He knew there was a regional loyalty common to all classes, a pride in coming from the old Mark of Brandenburg, or from Pomerania, or from Silesia, but he consistently scoffed at the first signs of Pan–Germanic sentiment among the bourgeoisie of his capital. To the popular writers of the Liberation era, Arndt and Fichte, Frederick was 'the un-German king', and his reputation went into eclipse until after the convulsion of 1848.

The 'Year of Revolutions' made few changes in Prussian society, but at least it permitted the middle classes to assert claims which would have seemed meaningless in the politics of Frederick's day. Yet the limited rights they secured did not go unchallenged; and in 1861 Frederick's great-great-nephew, William I, was locked in constitutional conflict with the Prussian legislature over parliamentary control of expenditure on the army. In defiance of the Deputies the King announced he would raise new regiments and, in January 1862 he insisted on presenting them with their Colours at a ceremony beside the tomb of Frederick II. This deliberate identification of the legendary Frederick with the political contests of a later age set a precedent which was to be followed throughout the Bismarckian Era (1862-90) and beyond. Eminent historians – Ranke, Droysen, Treitschke and Koser – represented Frederick as the King who had built up Prussia as the embryonic German State, in contrast to the multi-national and dynastic interests of Habsburg Austria. His ruthless and realistic diplomatic technique and the primacy he accorded the army over civil society were praised; his careful patronage of industry and husbandry was played down; his delight in French culture minimized. In 1866 Moltke's victory against the Austrians at Königgrätz (Sadowa) was celebrated by a solemn service of thanksgiving over Frederick's tomb, and so were the triumphs of 1870-1, which brought more French flags to be kept as trophies in the Garrison Church. The close association of the old King with the new Reich was emphasized

A photograph of Kaiser
William II dressing up as
Frederick the Great.

by Treitschke when, in 1879, he began to write his history of
nineteenth-century Germany: 'The twelve campaigns of the
Frederician Era have left their mark for ever on the martial spirit
of the Prussian people and the Prussian army', he wrote, 'Even
today, when discussing war, a north German involuntarily uses
the phrases of those halcyon days, speaking as Frederick did of
"brilliant manœuvres" and "lightning attacks".' And when the

218

centenary of the King's death was commemorated in 1866, William I – by now German Emperor as well as King of Prussia – virtually canonized his ancestor: 'Everything great and good blessing our Fatherland today rests upon the foundations which he laid', the old man declared.

The last Kaiser, William II, carried still further this adulation of the great Frederick, even at times dressing himself up in what he assumed to be the fashion of his great-great-great-great-uncle. The bicentenary of Frederick's birth was celebrated not, as it should have been, on 24 January 1912 but three days later, which happened to be William II's fifty-third birthday. Every student in Prussia was presented with a specially commissioned study of Frederick written by the Director of the State Archives and emphasizing the dynastic succession from the glories of the greatest Hohenzollern to the splendours of the Wilhelmine era. Later, in exile in the Netherlands, William II conceded that Frederick, for all his genius, possessed one defect – he admired the thought and literature of France and encouraged the Prussian people to share his delight in it, even though 'they lacked the mental toughness to resist its softening process'. But in 1912 the Kaiser's veneration for his ancestor was unbounded. There was some justification for the comment made by Lord Rosebery early in the First World War, that Frederick the Great had become 'the patron saint of Germany'.

With the fall of the Hohenzollerns in 1918 the Frederician legend was given a new perspective. The Versailles Treaty once again separated East Prussia from Brandenburg by a corridor of Polish land, and it became fashionable for politicians of the Centre and the Right to praise Frederick's eastern policy. To Hitler, dictating *Mein Kampf* to Rudolf Hess in prison at Landsberg during the summer of 1924, Frederick was 'the brilliant hero' who 'had in past times given the nation an elevated and resplendent symbol for all time to come'. Hitler was as anxious as William I and William II had been to establish the claim of his *Reich* to be the lineal descendant of the Frederician State, nonsensical though that might be, and it was Hitler himself who decided, soon after becoming Chancellor in 1933, that the opening of the first parliamentary session of his regime should be marked by a ceremony in the Garrison Church at Potsdam. Field-Marshal von Hindenburg, as Head of State, presided over the dedicatory service, which was held on 21 March: 'May the old spirit of this celebrated shrine permeate the generation of today', he declared, and after hearing an address of welcome from Hitler, he permitted his Chancellor

The dedicatory service at the Garrison Church in 1933, a propaganda exercise, designed to link Frederick to the Nazis. OPPOSITE President Hindenburg (*centre*), Hitler, and other Nazi leaders, while BELOW, underneath in the crypt, Frederick's coffin is draped with Nazi flags and wreaths.

to grasp him warmly by the hand. Then the octogenarian German President descended alone into the crypt to stand beside Frederick's remains as Napoleon and Alexander and all the Hohenzollern rulers had done before him. This time Hindenburg placed on the coffin a crown of laurel leaves in gold. The highly efficient propaganda machine of Dr Goebbels ensured that the whole episode was publicised widely at home and abroad. No one must doubt the continuity between Prussia's past and Germany's present: the cameras recorded a sentimental scene of political romanticism more worthy of a film-studio than a church.

This usurpation of the myth by the Third Reich was a historical confidence trick. Though Hitler and his henchmen practised some of the old King's diplomatic technique, the Greater Germany of Nazi ambition bore no resemblance to the carefully limited objectives of Frederick's policy. He had believed, as his political testaments show, in a balanced European order where a Greater Prussia would control the fulcrum of power but not absorb more lands than could be effectively accommodated within the existing state machine. It was Frederick's comparative moderation, together

with his persistence, which constituted his greatness as a statesman. Conceivably this code was the mainspring of Bismarck's
statecraft, but never of Hitler's. The officers who plotted against
the Nazi state were more truly custodians of the Prussian tradition
than was their Austrian-born Fuehrer.

Yet there is no doubt that in the catastrophic closing months of
the war, Hitler was heartened by his claim to be Frederick's distant
heir. He induced Goebbels to read to him passages from Carlyle's
massive biography of Frederick. The two doomed men so identified
the changing fortunes of the Seven Years' War with their own
predicament that, when they heard the unexpected news of
Roosevelt's death, they drew parallels with the sudden demise of
the Empress Elizabeth in the winter of 1761-2 and they hoped
American policy would change, just as Russia's had done nearly
two centuries before. But President Harry Truman was not Tsar
Peter III, nor was the White House a Winter Palace. The Allies
fought on and within three weeks Hitler shot himself in his bunker.
It is recorded that the Fuehrer's underground study had on its
walls only one painting, a portrait of Frederick the Great.

Frederick the Great. Is there
anything left of the man,
and the power he wielded
beyond the bleak stone of an
equestrian statue?

ST. JOSEPH'S COLLEGE OF EDUCATION
TRENCH HOUSE
BELFAST 11

Further Reading

The most revealing sources for seeking to understand Frederick are his own writings. I have made use of the *Oeuvres de Frederic le Grand*, edited by J.D.E. Preuss (30 volumes, Berlin 1846-56) and his *Politische Correspondenz* (47 volumes, Berlin 1879-1939). I have also used an edition of his *Military Instructions* (London 1797).

Books in English include:

Carlyle, Thomas, *History of Frederick II of Prussia* (London, 1899, and other editions)

Craig, Gordon A., *The Politics of the Prussian Army* (New York, 1955)

Easum, Chester V., *Prince Henry of Prussia* (Madison, 1942)

Flenley, Ralph, *Modern German History* (London, 1968)

Flint, F.S., *Frederick the Great, the Memoirs of his Reader, Henri de Catt* (London, 1916)

Gaxotte, Pierre, *Frederick the Great* (London, 1941)

Gooch, G.P., *Frederick the Great* (London, 1947)

Horn, D.B., *Frederick the Great and the Rise of Prussia* (London, 1964)

Lavisse, E., *The Youth of Frederick the Great* (London, 1891)

Lodge, Sir Richard, *Studies in Eighteenth Century Diplomacy* (London, 1930)

Macartney, C.A. (ed.), *The Habsburg and Hohenzollern Dynasties in the Seventeenth and Eighteenth Centuries* (New York, 1970)

Mitford, Nancy, *Frederick the Great* (London, 1970)

Nicolson, Sir Harold, *The Age of Reason* (London, 1960)

Paret, Peter (ed.), *Frederick the Great* (London, 1972)

Reiners, Ludwig, *Frederick the Great* (London, 1960)

Ritter, Gerhard, *Frederick the Great* (London, 1968)

Simon, Edith, *The Making of Frederick the Great* (London, 1963)

Wilhelmina, Margravine of Bayreuth, *Memoirs* (London, 1812)

Wright, Constance, *A Royal Affinity* (London, 1967)

Zimmermann, H., *Dr Zimmermann's Conversations with the Late King of Prussia* (London, 1791)

List of Illustrations

Index

L 2621
4B S
£ 3·25